This is France

I C Thimann
formerly Chief Language Master, Nottingham High School

M F R Whalley
County Inspector for Modern Languages, Essex

EUROPEAN
SCHOOLBOOKS
HATIER

Acknowledgements

We should like to express our grateful thanks to the many people who have helped us to produce this book.

We are particularly grateful to the French Government Tourist Office and French Railways in this country and to Documentation Française and the Institut National de Recherche et de Documentation Pédagogique in France who have been so generous in supplying photographs.

We should also like to thank "Food from France" and the firms of Renault, Citroën and Michelin as well as all the individual photographers whose names appear alongside their photographs.

Finally our thanks to Mademoiselle Françoise Guillot and Monsieur Jacques Pierre for the research they have done on our behalf.

Illustrations by Nick Jones

ISBN 0 85048 030 2

Printed in England by McCorquodale (Newton) Limited, Merseyside.

Contents

Preface

France is our nearest neighbour. For almost a thousand years France and England have been closely linked together. For four hundred years after the Norman conquest in 1066, the kings of England were also dukes of France – of Anjou, Poitou, Aquitaine, the Auvergne. French queens sat on the English throne, and in the course of a centuries-long struggle for power French kings married English (or Scottish) princesses.

The rivalries of the past have given way to the "entente cordiale" which has grown up between the two countries in the twentieth century. In two world wars France and Britain fought side by side as staunch allies, and today in the wider context of the European Economic Community they pursue their common aim in the hope of creating a better Europe.

So it is important for us to know something about this country, the largest in western Europe, and something about the people who live there. This book will help you to explore some aspects of the country. You can find out more for yourself by following the suggestions made in the Projects section of each chapter. France has so much to offer, there is so much to explore and discover. This is just a beginning.

Fernand Marty

Food and drink

Seven o'clock in any French town on a weekday morning. The average French family is already having breakfast. A long working day lies ahead. Work in most offices and factories begins at eight a.m. and schools start at eight or half-past.

Is this why the French eat such a light breakfast? Perhaps it's difficult to be very hungry so early in the morning. They eat rolls or crusty French bread spread with jam, not marmalade, and have bowls or large cups of hot milky coffee or chocolate to drink.

Don't think the French ill-mannered if you see them dip their rolls into their coffee. It's the normal thing to do. They eat vast amounts of bread which they buy fresh each day at the baker's. There are no bread — or milk — deliveries. There are many different kinds of bread to choose from. 'Croissants' are the popular but expensive crescent-shaped rolls, and the commonest of the long thin French loaves is known as a 'baguette'.

The French work through till mid-day usually without even a mid-morning snack. No wonder

A French breakfast

then that the lunch hour is a long one, lasting from twelve till two, and lunch itself an important meal.

A Frenchman may well whet his appetite by popping into a café for a leisurely 'apéritif' with his friends on his way home for lunch.

The first course, the 'hors d'œuvre', may be 'pâté' or 'charcuterie', a slice of melon or a salad of grated carrots and mayonnaise, and there is always crusty bread and a bottle of ordinary table wine on the table. The main course is usually meat, perhaps steak and salad. It may be horse meat which is cheaper than beef and a popular substitute. There are special butcher's shops which sell only horse-meat. You can recognise them by their shop sign — a horse's head, usually in gilt, over the door.

Sappa

A 'boucherie chevaline'

Vegetables, for example 'haricots verts', are eaten separately, after the main course, but on the same plate and using the same knife and fork, and there is nearly always a green salad to follow, tossed in a garlic-flavoured oil and vinegar dressing.

Young children may drink squash with their meal though it is expensive. Coca-cola is more likely, or wine diluted with water. The French do not drink much water straight from the tap. They prefer a bottle of mineral water — this is the water from natural springs which is generally supposed to help them digest their rather rich food.

Food from France

The cheese course comes next and there are about three hundred different sorts of cheese in France for the housewife to choose from. It has been said that she could serve a different kind every day of the year. Cheese is always eaten with bread, never with biscuits.

There will not be a pudding, although there might be a flaky French pastry or a fruit tart on Sunday or for a birthday or other special occasion. Lunch normally finishes with fruit and coffee.

After lunch it's back to work from two o'clock until six or even seven. There is no afternoon tea, but when the children come home from school just after five, they will usually have a snack — probably a drink of milk and a piece of bread or a bun and bar of chocolate. Now is the best time for any homework, for when father arrives home about seven o'clock the rest of the evening could well be spent at table. Dinner is the time when the whole family is together exchanging the day's news, and there is never any shortage of conversation.

Top: *Various mineral waters*
Bottom: *A selection of French cheeses*

Meals on very special occasions can last up to four or five hours. If you are invited out to an evening meal, you are in for a pleasant surprise. Take along a small offering of chocolates or flowers for your hostess who has probably spent most of the day in the kitchen.

The dinner will start either with a tureen of home-made soup or an elaborate hors d'œuvre. There may be fish before the main meat course. The vegetables too may be the less familiar ones like chicory, aubergines, artichokes or asparagus. Each dish is served with a carefully prepared home-made sauce, and there is a different wine with each of the main courses. There will be a choice of several kinds of cheese and finally a large bowl or basket of fruit will appear on the table. Fruit is plentiful, varied and relatively cheap. In the warm climate of the south it is possible to grow peaches and nectarines, grapes and figs, as well as the more usual apples, plums and pears, so the fruit bowl can look very attractive.

By and large then, the French have two substantial meals a day — lunch and dinner. Breakfast is light and there is very little 'nibbling' between meals.

Now that more and more French housewives are going out to work, they have less time to spend in the kitchen preparing food. So the use of convenience foods such as packet soups, tinned vegetables, frozen fish fingers, is becoming more widespread.

Another change is occurring. In Paris especially, but also in other large cities, the journey to work is often long and tiring. It isn't easy to get home for lunch even with a two-hour lunch break. So more people are working 'une

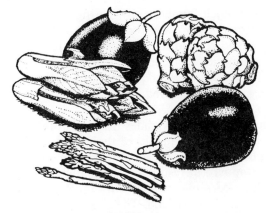

journée continue'. This means that they have only a short lunch break, and finish work an hour or so earlier. This gives them a longer evening to enjoy at home. They can get 'un wimpy' or 'un hamburger' or a light dish like an omelette in a snack-bar or self-service restaurant. If you see a sign saying 'On peut apporter son manger', you can take in your own food and simply buy your wine there. In fact French workers often have 'sandwiches' for their lunch. Pieces of fresh, crusty bread are broken off from a 'baguette', liberally spread with cheese or pâté and swilled down with ample quantities of red wine.

Sappa

Top: *Chicory, aubergines, artichokes, and asparagus.*
Bottom: *The mid-day break*

Most French families enjoy eating out and do so as often as they can afford it. It is difficult nowadays to find somewhere cheap to eat — say, a meal under 12 francs — but it is not at all difficult to find good quality food well cooked and attractively served.

The Michelin guide grades the best hotels according to the quality of their food. As it is published each year every effort is made to keep the standard of restaurant meals high and perhaps earn one of Michelin's much coveted rosettes for good food. The chef of a good hotel takes a tremendous pride in the meals he serves to his clients and jealously guards his reputation. One famous chef in Louis XIV's time committed suicide because the fish he needed for a royal banquet did not arrive in time. Though present-day chefs would hardly go to such extreme lengths, they regard it as a great disgrace if their hotel is down-graded by the Michelin inspectors.

Many restaurants, especially in the provinces, are family concerns. They take a genuine pride in their cooking and service and treat their clients like old friends.

By law, every restaurant has to display its menu and prices. You need to understand these if you want to make the most of eating out. There are two basic types of menu — the menu 'à prix fixe' sometimes called 'menu touristique' and the 'menu à la carte'.

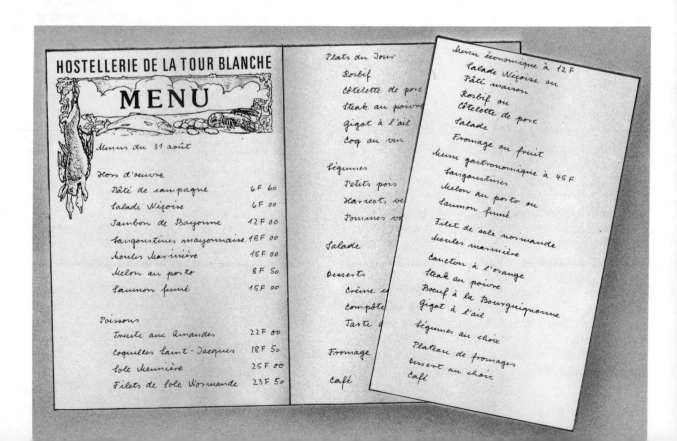

HOSTELLERIE DE LA TOUR BLANCHE

MENU

Menus du 31 août

Hors d'oeuvre

Pâté de campagne	6 F 60
Salade Niçoise	6 F 00
Jambon de Bayonne	12 F 00
Langoustines mayonnaise	18 F 00
Moules Marinière	15 F 00
Melon au porto	8 F 50
Saumon fumé	15 F 00

Poissons

Truite aux Amandes	22 F 00
Coquilles Saint-Jacques	18 F 50
Sole Meunière	25 F 00
Filets de Sole Normande	23 F 50

Plats du Jour
Rosbif
Côtelette de porc
Steak au poivre
Gigot à l'ail
Coq au vin

Légumes
Petits pois
Haricots ve
Pommes v

Salade

Desserts
Crème
Compôte
Tarte

Fromage

Café

Menu économique à 12 F
Salade Niçoise ou
Pâté maison
Rosbif ou
Côtelette de porc
Salade
Fromage ou fruit

Menu gastronomique à 45 F
Langoustines
Melon au porto ou
Saumon fumé
Filet de sole normande
Moules marinière
Caneton à l'orange
Steak au poivre
Boeuf à la Bourguignonne
Gigot à l'ail
Légumes au choix
Plateau de fromages
Dessert au choix
Café

The fixed price menu means that the restaurant offers you a set meal at a set price. You know in advance exactly how much the meal is going to cost. If the menu is marked 'Service non compris' or 'Service 15%', you are expected to give a tip of 15% which will be added to your bill at the end of the meal. You will have to pay extra for any drinks you have unless, as is sometimes the case, the fixed price menu includes a small carafe of 'vin ordinaire'.

If you want to choose your own menu, you must eat 'à la carte'. Each item is priced separately. This way the meal costs more, but you have a wide choice and get exactly what you want.

Another extra may be the 'couvert' − the cover charge to meet the cost of the fresh paper table-cloth, the spotlessly clean napkins and the bread which is always on the table.

If you are ordering steak, the waiter will ask you how you like it done, whether you want it 'saignant', that is very red with the blood still running from it, 'à point', still red in the middle but cooked rather longer, 'bien cuit', well done, or even 'très bien cuit', very well done.

Try anything and everything that you can. The French diet, contrary to popular belief, does not consist of snails and frogs' legs − these are delicacies which you will usually only find on the menu of a good restaurant. France has a wonderful reputation for her food. One of the adventures of a holiday in France can be exploring the variety of her 'cuisine'.

The French spend a much larger proportion of their family income on food and drink than most nations. They also consume on average more alcohol than any other nation in the world. This, together with the rich food, causes many of them to suffer from liver complaints. So the spa towns have never lost their popularity. There the French hope to win back their health by strict dieting and 'taking the waters'.

The breathalyser (l'alcotest) is used by the French police. Since wine is such an important part of French meals, drivers find it difficult

Anti-drink posters

sometimes not to drink and drive. You can get a drink at a motorway restaurant too. But advertisements for alcohol are not permitted on T.V. and you will see posters urging you not to drive if you have had too much to drink.

Various measures to improve the situation are talked about − reducing the price of soft drinks for example. (They are very expensive.) There has even been talk of introducing licensing laws − so far unknown in France.

Projects

1 What would you buy in the following shops?
boucherie chevaline, pâtisserie, charcuterie,
boulangerie.

2 These are some of the different courses in a French
dinner. They are not in the right order. Re-arrange
them in the order in which they would appear on the
menu.
café, salade, dessert, digestif, rôti, entrée, hors d'œuvre,
apéritif, fruits, fromage.

3 Here are some French terms we use in connection with
cooking and food. What do they mean?
soufflé, purée, sauté, flambé, cordon bleu, à votre
santé, maître d'hôtel, bon appétit.

4 What would you be getting if you had:
a crêpes, b crudités, c coq au vin, d ratatouille,
e œuf à la coque, f cuisses de grenouille.

5 What is the difference between English and French
'prunes', and English and French 'raisins'?

6 How did 'blancmange' get its name? Do you like 'éclairs'?
Can you think of anything else you eat which has a
French name?

7 Make up a menu based on French food for a meal
which you would enjoy eating.

8 Here are some regional dishes. Find out what they are
and from which region they come.
a bouillabaisse, b choucroute, c quiche,
d cousse-cousse, e bœuf bourguignonne, f homard à
l'armoricaine.

9 Here are the names of various kinds of French bread.
Draw them to show the difference in their shapes and
label them.
croissants, baguettes, flûtes, ficelles, petits pains,
brioches, bâtard, couronne.

10 You have been out for a meal. The 'à la carte' menu has
cost you 35 francs, but then you notice that the cover
charge is 3 francs and there is 15% to add on for service.
You give the waiter a hundred franc note. How much
change will you get?
You have chosen a 'menu à prix fixe' at 15F. It was
marked 'Boisson non comprise, service compris'. You
had a 5F carafe of red wine with your meal and the
waiter gives you a bill for 23F. Is this correct?

11 Here is a simple French recipe. What dish is being made?
Why not try to make it yourself when you get home?

100 gr granulated sugar
3 tablespoons water
3 egg yolks
½ litre milk
1 tablespoon castor sugar
A few drops vanilla essence.

Make a caramel of the granulated sugar and water.
When it is a rich brown colour, coat the bottom of a
mould with it. Beat together the egg yolks, castor sugar
and vanilla essence, add the warmed milk and pour into
the mould. Stand the mould in a dish of water and
bake in a moderate oven until it has set. Turn out on to
a serving dish and eat cold.

12 What is the meaning of VDQS and 'appellation
contrôlée'? Copy the shapes of the different French wine
bottles and find out which wine is bottled in each of
them.

13 Make a map of the principal wine-growing areas of
France. Include Champagne, the Loire, Bordeaux, the
Rhône, Alsace and Burgundy. Put in also on your map
the main spa towns.

14 From the Guide Michelin (you can see one at the
public library) find the names of some hotels and
restaurants in the following towns. Which restaurant in
each town offers an especially good meal? See if you can
work out what the 'spécialité' of each of the
restaurants is.
Grenoble, Chartres, Carcassonne, Bordeaux, Tours,
Arles.

For your folder
Make a collection of labels from food packets and wine
bottles which have French names on them.
Make a collage picture of French food from magazine
advertisements.
Collect recipes for French dishes.

Schools

A primary school class at work

I.N.R.D.P. (Jean Suquet)

No school on Wednesday mornings, perhaps the whole day free, no school uniforms, no morning assembly — these are probably the things about French schools which English pupils first notice when they go to France on their exchange visits. But on the other side of the coin — the idea of school on Saturday mornings, school starting at eight or half-past in the morning, and going on till five or six in the evening is not nearly so appealing.

So just what is going to school like for young people in France?

French children can go to school from the age of two. France has a high proportion of working mothers and the provision of nursery schools is good. Even where the mother does not go out to work, she may decide to send her two or three year old to the 'école maternelle' to learn to mix with other children and have fun playing with them.

The 'école maternelle' takes children at any time between the ages of two and six, and until the final year there are no 'ordinary' lessons at all, just activities like painting, singing and dancing. After lunch the smallest children have a rest in their cots — their siesta time. These nursery schools stay open even during the long summer holiday and offer a chance to girl students to earn some pocket-money.

School is compulsory from the age of six, and from six to eleven children go to the primary school (école primaire). They have a long day, from half-past eight in the morning until half-past four in the afternoon, but there are two hours off for lunch when those who can do so go home. Lessons are rather formal and are more or less the same all over France. The 'instituteur' or 'institutrice', trained at an 'école normale', concentrates on correct speaking and writing in French. Slang heard on the 'télé' is very strongly disapproved of. There is no corporal punishment, no uniform, except the pinafores which most French children wear for practical reasons, and no religious instruction in state schools.

Then at the age of eleven most children go to a C.E.S. (Collège d'Enseignement Secondaire), a comprehensive school of at least six hundred pupils. The first year of the C.E.S. is the 'sixième', the second the 'cinquième' and so on. At the end of the 'troisième', when he is fifteen, a pupil can sit for the B.E.P.C. (Brevet d'Enseignement Premier Cycle) and this is the end of the first cycle of his education.

11

	8h	9h	10h	11h	12h	2h	3h	4h	5h	6h
Lundi	Math	Philosophie	Physique	Histoire		Anglais	Math		Allemand	
Mardi	Math	Sciences Naturelles		Sciences Naturelles		Chimie		Gymnastique		
Mercredi	Math	Géographie	Philosophie	Physique						
Jeudi	Géographie	Anglais	Philosophie	Physique		Math	Histoire	Allemand	Gymnastique	
Vendredi	Allemand		Philosophie	Math		Devoir	Devoir	Devoir	Devoir	
Samedi	Chimie		Sciences Naturelles							

So far the pattern has been very much the same for most French children, except that those who are good at school work have been in Section 1 of the C.E.S. studying a wide range of subjects pretty thoroughly, whereas the programme has been modified for those in Sections 2 and 3. All through this 'premier cycle' a 'conseil d'orientation' (a body giving advice on courses and careers) will have been watching each pupil's progress, and their recommendation will decide what he does next.

At fifteen, the ablest pupils will transfer to a Lycée – nowadays a sort of Sixth Form College – and prepare for the Baccalauréat, an exam which they will take three years later. Other pupils will go to a C.E.T. (Collège d'Enseignement Technique) and follow a two-year course in more practical subjects like building or carpentry, dressmaking or typing, mechanical or electrical engineering. At the end of this course they will take either the C.A.P. (Certificat d'Aptitude Professionnelle) or the

more difficult B.E.P. (Brevet d'Etudes Professionnelles). Some pupils of course will leave school as soon as they are sixteen and look for a job straight away.

Pupils who live in a rural district will probably not go to a C.E.S. as the area may not be big enough to warrant one. Unless they wish to be boarders at a C.E.S. some distance from their homes, they will go to to a C.E.G. (Collège d'Enseignement Général) or to a lycée in the nearest town. These provincial lycées still take pupils right through from 11 to 18 instead of taking them at 15 as the big lycées in Paris and the large towns do.

The French lycées are proud of their traditions. They make the 'lycéens' work very hard during the three years (deuxième, première and terminale) before the Baccalauréat – usually referred to by the pupils as the 'Bac' – which they take at about the age of eighteen. There are few clubs, societies, or team games. French parents prefer a star pupil to a star footballer.

The 'Bac' is the school-leaving examination for lycéens, and those who pass are entitled to go to a university. There are eight different types of Bac (five at the 'lycée classique' and three at the 'lycée technique'). Each involves eight or nine subjects, either written or oral. There is no early specialisation. French, mathematics, a foreign language and 'philo' (philosophy) are compulsory, and nowadays the mark in physical education can count towards the Bac. This, it is hoped, will make physical education more worthwhile in the eyes of the pupils.

The Bac is a frightening challenge to all French students – even the most brilliant. They need an overall average of 60% – 'douze de moyenne' –

Sappa

Top: *A science student's time-table for the final year*
Bottom: *'Break' at a large Paris lycée*

Student demonstration in '68

in order to pass. If they manage between 40% and 60% their summer holiday may be delayed for a couple of weeks until they have taken an oral test in the subjects in which they failed. If they don't pass 'l'Oral' they will have to do the whole exam again the following year.

Some of the biggest lycées have as many as three thousand pupils. Their most able students can go on after their Bac to a special school which prepares them for careers in government, the diplomatic service, the army, the stock exchange and top jobs in the commercial world. These schools are called the 'grandes écoles'. Entrance is by competitive examination and the qualifications they give are very highly prized. If you have been to 'Polytechnique' or the E.N.A. ('Ecole Nationale d'Administration') or the H.E.C. ('Hautes Etudes Commerciales') you are well on the way to a first-class career.

In 1968 the educational system in France seemed on the point of breakdown. Students and lycéens were noisily demanding reforms. 'Participation' was a key word. One of the results of their protests was the creation of school councils. Pupils — one from each senior class — teachers, parents and the headteacher meet in the 'conseil d'administration' to discuss school policy. Pupils may make suggestions. At one C.E.S. they suggested that if boys and girls had lunch together, manners would improve — and they did! There is also a joint 'conseil de discipline' and a court of appeal, at which pupils accused of serious offences can actually be represented by a lawyer if they choose to.

France has no schools like the ancient and famous British public schools, but outside the state system there are many Catholic schools, the 'écoles libres', where priests and nuns still teach, and the pupils *do* wear uniform. Even so, their teaching, except in religion, and their exams are controlled by the Ministry of Education.

The Ministry of Education decides what is to be taught in French schools, what form exams and school reports shall take; it fixes the hours of work and the dates of school holidays. It has always 'run' everything. It has advisers and inspectors in twenty-four regions up and down the country to see that the education service is running smoothly. These regions are called 'académies' and at the centre of each is a university town, like Lille, Amiens or Paris itself.

13

Here are some real life examples to give you an idea how the system works.

Pascal wants to be a farmer, so after his B.E.P.C. he went to a technical lycée where he is working for his Bac in agriculture. If he had been less ambitious he could have gone to a C.E.T., and taken a far less demanding course.

Yvette is a hairdresser — she went to a C.E.T. in Tours, her home town, and learned her trade there.

Guy always hated school. He was in Section 3 at his C.E.S. and never learned a thing until he went as an apprentice builder to a special school for difficult and backward pupils. He now has a job on a building site.

Jean-Marc wants to be a motor mechanic, so he did his training at a C.E.T. in Marseille. He is now doing his military service, earlier than he need, so that he can get it out of the way and settle down to a job without interruption when he gets back.

Véronique is going to be an archaeologist. She passed her Bac at a Paris lycée and is now at the Sorbonne studying Latin, Greek and ancient history.

Stéphane intends to become a civil engineer and as he is a brilliant student he is having special coaching and trying to get into one of the 'grandes écoles', preferably the 'Ecole Normale Supérieure des Ponts et Chaussées'.

Projects

1 Find the odd man out.
   a C.E.S., lycée, école maternelle, B.E.P.C., C.E.G.
   b déjeuner, réfectoire, dortoir, cour, salle de classe.
   c chant, travaux manuels, bibliothèque, français, dessin.

2 Here are some slang words which you would be sure to hear in a French school. Can you discover what they mean?
   prof, pion, boulot, bachot, une colle, potasser, dingue, la loco . . .

3 Set out your school time-table in French. How does it compare with a French pupil's 'Emploi du Temps'?

4 List any further facts you have found out about French schools, whether from books, visits, or from a French pen-friend.

5 What are the following: classes de neige? the 'Grandes Ecoles'? a 'Conseil de Discipline? an 'Ecole Libre'? the 'Académies'?

6 André is in the cinquième at a C.E.S. Which year would he be in if he were at an English school? Which year would a pupil of fifteen be in at a French school?

7 True or false?
   a The Sorbonne is a lycée in Paris.
   b A 'normalien' is a person training to be a teacher.
   c An 'inspecteur d'académie' is a person who inspects academies.

8 Georges plans to become a nuclear physicist; Anne-Marie is going to a university to study languages; Alain wants to be a motor mechanic. Make a diagram showing the type of schools each would go to and the number of years he would spend in each.

To discuss
What do you consider to be the good and bad points of the French educational system?
Is early specialisation a good or a bad thing?

Sport

A rugby match: Brive v. Béziers

Presse Sports

Football

France 5 England 2!

What sport could that be? It was on a February evening in Paris in 1963 that England's soccer team were knocked out of the European Nations' Cup by that score. Two months later Sir Alf Ramsey became manager of England who in 1966 beat France 2-0 on their way to winning the World Cup. France came bottom of their group and failed even to qualify for the Mexico 1970 or the Germany 1974 World Cup.

No French club has won a European cup competition yet. Few, if any French footballers or clubs are well known abroad. In the 1972-3 season some French footballers even went on strike. Although it is the most widely played game of all in France, football is under a cloud and in urgent need of a dynamic leader.

Rugby

In contrast France has done very well in Rugby Union, winning the International Championship in 1967 and again in 1970. The team has a tradition of open, exciting play. Televised internationals have helped to make the game more popular.

Rugby League is played mainly in the south-west of France where it has tremendous popular appeal.

Pelota

This area, the Basque region, is also the home of 'pelota', the fastest ball game in the world. The ball, a little smaller than a cricket ball but just as hard, often travels at an incredible speed. The players wear a 'chistera', a kind of wicker glove that is half bat, half basket. With this they hurl the ball against a high wall at the end of a huge open court. The wall is made of granite to withstand the impact. The basic idea of the game is to strike the ball so hard against the wall that it ricochets off out of your opponent's reach.

Pelota players in action

Pétanque

Also connected with the south is 'pétanque', a kind of bowls, which in a slightly different version is played throughout France. The players flick metal bowls into the air and try to land nearest the marker, a small white ball called the 'cochonnet'. A leisurely, relaxing game, it is often played during the lunch-hour on a firm, sandy piece of ground in a public park. To enthusiasts it can be intensely competitive and exciting. Perhaps in mood it is the nearest thing the French have to the game of cricket, which is unknown in France.

Individual sports

The French are well known to be individualists — they like to 'do their own thing'. And with higher wages, a shorter working week and more leisure they can do their own thing more and more. Sailing, ski-ing, riding, underwater exploration are all growing rapidly in popularity year by year. They are all sports which people can practise and enjoy on holiday or during a long weekend, without belonging to an organised team. Every year, for instance, there are an estimated 100,000 more Frenchmen taking to the ski-slopes, adding up now to a probable three million skiers in France.

It is hardly surprising then that it is in such individual sports that the French have gained their outstanding successes of recent years.

In the 1968 Winter Olympics held in Grenoble, Jean-Claude Killy became a national hero, winning gold medals in all three alpine ski events. Now retired from ski-ing, he is trying to make a name for himself as a film star!

Eric Tabarly won the single-handed transatlantic yacht race in 1964 in his yacht Pen-Duick II. This race, organised by the 'Observer' takes place every four years. In 1968 however, Tabarly in Pen-Duick IV, the favourite, collided with another boat shortly after leaving Plymouth. Then Alain Colas appeared on the scene. Many people thought the trimaran too big and unsafe in the Atlantic, but not Alain Colas. He spent all his savings on a seventy foot long three-hulled boat. In 1972, with his boat stocked with food given to him by farmers from his native Normandy, Colas won the race in a time of 20½ days. The first three to reach America were all French, and Colas had beaten the old record by 5½ days.

Presse Sports

Fernand M

Top: *A game of 'pétanque'*
Bottom: *Down-hill ski: Fabienne Serrai*

Left:
*'Export 33' – round
the world race 1973*

Below:
*Mountain stage of the
Tour de France*

The Tour de France

A somewhat quicker form of transport – the
cycle – becomes the absorbing interest for
Frenchmen in late June and early July. It is then
that the 'Tour de France' takes place. This cycle
race around France lasts about three weeks. It is
divided into daily stages. (Some of these take
place in neighbouring countries – over the
cobblestones of Belgium or the mountains of
Switzerland, and in 1975 there was a stage in the
south of England.) Into every village and town it
brings a fever of excitement. The riders cover
about three thousand miles in the course of this
gruelling race, which takes them right from
northern France to the steep mountain passes of
the southern stages.

The first race in 1903 was sponsored by a sports
magazine, and nowadays two newspapers are the
sponsors. One of these, 'L'Equipe,' has the largest
circulation of any daily sports newspaper in the
world. The race itself is surrounded by publicity.
The riders, of whom there are usually about a
hundred and thirty, race in teams sponsored by
business firms, wearing the name of their team
on their shirts. Publicity cars precede the riders
on each stage to advertise a particular drink or
make of tyre to the waiting crowds lining the
route. As the riders pass by, all eyes will be on
two men – the local hero, who will be making a
special effort to win the stage in his home region
and qualify for the green jersey of the stage
winner, and the overall leader who wears the
distinctive yellow jersey, the 'maillot jaune'.

Riders have to be dedicated and determined.
The Tour is exhausting. Strict rules are observed
over drugs, especially since the tragic death of
Tommy Simpson, the most successful Briton to
ride in the race.

Rainger Stride and Jones – Architects

Stands at Longchamps race-course

Motor racing

Probably the two best known events in the car racing calendar are the Monte Carlo Rally and the '24-heures' at Le Mans.

The Monte Carlo Rally is held in January. Groups of cars start from various cities all over Europe (Athens, Stockholm, Dover) and make their way, often through snow, ice, rain and fog, to Monte Carlo. Here the drivers with the fewest penalty points take part in a further series of road-trials to decide the overall winner.

The 24-hour Le Mans is one of the most exciting highlights of the season. It takes place over an eight and a half mile circuit, which includes two

The 24-hours at Le Mans

Presse Sports

hairpin bends and an S-bend. Starting usually at 4 p.m. on a Saturday in June, cars drive through the night, stopping only to re-fuel and to change drivers. On the fastest sections of the circuit cars reach over 300 k.p.h.

Horse racing

An equally famous race-track, but this time for horse racing is Longchamps on the outskirts of Paris. Lester Piggott has often ridden winners here in the big Sunday races, and French horses are often equally successful in Britain. Thousands of Frenchmen bet on the state-sponsored 'tiercé' each week — they have to forecast the first three horses past the post in a particular race. The result, together with the amount of the prize money, is always announced on the radio news.

The government and sport

The Government makes money from sport through the 'tiercé', but it provides massive financial aid for sport as well.

When France failed to win a single gold medal in the 1960 Olympics in Rome, it was a severe blow to her national pride. A national plan was drawn up to provide more sports-grounds, gymnasia, swimming-pools and so on.

Before the 1968 Olympics in Mexico a special sports centre was built at Font-Romeu in the Pyrenees, so that athletes could train under comparatively high-altitude conditions more like those they would expect to find in Mexico. British Olympic athletes as well as French used the centre for their training. The French won seven gold medals in Mexico.

But it is not only international athletes who have benefited. Grenoble's magnificent ice-rink built for the winter Olympics is used by the ordinary townspeople. Thanks to government grants, thousands of French school-children, many of them from the Paris region, spend one of the winter months in the mountains. They have lessons in the mornings, and 'snow sports' in the afternoons.

In secondary schools now, pupils have three hours of physical education and two hours of open-air sports activities per week. Inter-school matches are rare, but any young person can join a local sports club and so take part in matches, often on Wednesday afternoons when there is no school.

French youth today has more sports facilities than any previous generation. Will a fitter, more active and sports-minded population be the result? The Government hopes so.

Projects

1 Has a stage of the Tour de France ever taken place in Britain? If so, where?

2 What English game would you say is the nearest to pelota?

3 What are the following sports called in English? le cross, le rugby à treize, le catch, les courses hippiques, la natation.

4 Find out in which sports the following French people are famous.
Yves St-Martin, Colette Besson, Jean-Pierre Beltoise, Michel Rousseau, Isabelle Mir, Fabienne Serrat.

5 In January, draw in on your map the routes to be taken to Monte-Carlo by the competitors from the various starting-points.

6 In June, draw the route for this year's Tour de France. Mark off the daily stages, noting distances.

7 Try to get hold of a copy of 'L'Equipe'. Make a list of the sporting terms which are common to French and English.

8 On your map of France mark the places which have First Division football teams. Compare the distances teams have to travel to away games with distances in Britain.

9 Note down month by month the sporting events in France and make an illustrated calendar of them.

To discuss
Is it still true that the French are better at individual sports than they are at team games? If so, why is this? At what sports have they been particularly successful?

For your folder
In January, collect newspaper reports, photographs and results of the Monte-Carlo rally.
In June, collect similar details of the 24-hour Le Mans.
In June/July, collect details of the Tour de France.

19

Private cars

Documentation Française

France is more than twice the size of Britain, yet she has fewer inhabitants. There are fewer large cities, and distances between them are often great. Thus the private car has a most important place in French transport. Car ownership (per head of the population) is higher than in either Britain or West Germany. Add the pioneering work of the French in the development of the motor-car and it is easy to see why the average Frenchman loves his car so much.

Amongst the earliest pioneers two are still household names today – PEUGEOT and RENAULT.

Armand Peugeot began by building tricycles and bicycles and one of the Peugeot group of companies still makes cycles and motorcycles. In 1888 Armand designed a steam-driven tricycle and in 1890 a car with a paraffin engine, gear-box and solid rubber tyres. This vehicle *followed* the Paris – Brest – Paris cycle race; it couldn't catch the cyclists! It covered the 680 miles at an average speed of 8 m.p.h. Strangely enough, the origins of Michelin, the French tyre manufacturers, go back to cycling. One day in 1918 two Michelin brothers helped a cyclist to repair

his punctured tyre. It wasn't easy, since the tyre was glued to the wheel. This incident led to the brothers' invention of a detachable pneumatic tyre.

By 1898 Peugeot had three factories building five hundred cars a year (they now produce 2,400 a day, or one every 30 seconds). This was the year in which Louis Renault built his first motorcar in a shed in the grounds of his father's house, near Paris.

Car races such as Paris – Nice, Paris – Bordeaux, were staged and gave an ideal opportunity for publicising this new form of transport to the man in the street and the industry grew rapidly.

The First World War (1914-18) interrupted this expansion. Shells, guns, army lorries and later

Documentation Française

Renault

Top left: *Peugeot 'Break' 1894*
Top right: *The taxis of the Marne*
Bottom: *Renault works at Flins*

Bibliothèque Nationale

aircraft engines and light tanks were made in the factories instead of cars. Renault taxi-cabs rushed Allied soldiers to the front during the battle of the Marne in 1914. The soldiers nick-named them 'the taxis of the Marne'.

The two other present-day French motor companies were founded between the two World Wars.

André Citroën produced his first mass-production model in 1919. To show how good his cars were, André organised great motor-rallies all over the world. A Citroën expedition crossed the Sahara desert in 1922-3 and a few years later a similar expedition starting from the Mediterranean coast of Asia crossed the Himalayan mountains and the Gobi desert to reach the China sea.

Renault

Citroën brought many new ideas to the car industry — it provided its customers with cut-rate insurance, made use of aircraft trailing streamers to advertise its cars, and drove its cars over a cliff to show how solid they were!

The SIMCA company at first produced Fiat models under licence before launching its first model in 1936.

All the companies suffered in the Second World War. The Germans took control of many of the factories. The allies destroyed 80% of Renault's factory in Paris in air-raids. By the end of the war in 1945, 40% of all private cars had been destroyed.

Gradually the factories began to produce cars again — at first the pre-war models, then new mass-production types to meet the growing demand. Renault, the largest manufacturer, was nationalised by the French government. Many of the smaller firms, who had built luxury or sports cars before the war, disappeared, often taken over by the larger companies. More than 200,000 people work for Renault, the country's largest industrial employer.

Mass-production was the key to success. Peugeot built a million of its 403 model, Simca a million 'Arondes', and Renault in the space of four years a million 'Dauphines'. The era of family and pleasure motoring had arrived.

Citroën's 2 CV (cheval-vapeur) with its distinctive, almost 'home-made' look, was the first car to hit the real mass market. It was absolutely basic, cheap and immensely popular. Their DS range, with superb springing and a chassis which could be raised for travelling over bumpy roads, was designed for the luxury end of the market.

Top: *Citroën's 2CV*
Bottom: *Production line at Renault*

Citroën took over the Panhard company in 1965 and after entering into agreements with the German firm NSU to develop a new type of engine, and with the Italian sports-car firm of Maserati to build a GT car, began to work closely with the Italian company Fiat.

Simca, like the Rootes company in Britain, was taken over by the American firm Chrysler. The Chrysler 2-litre was a joint Franco-British production, as is the Alpine, designed at Coventry but built in France and exported to Britain.

Peugeot and Renault co-operate closely on research. Together they have built a track for high-speed tests, and they manufacture certain parts jointly. Their luxury saloons, the Renault 30 and the Peugeot 604 have the same engine.

Export sales have continued to increase in importance and assembly and production plants are scattered world-wide. Simca exports over 60% of its production, Citroën about 50%. Renault is one of the major exporters of cars to Britain. The oil crisis and inflation of the mid-seventies made the small car popular. Not only was it cheaper to buy but it was also cheaper to run. French manufacturers were not as hard hit as many others because they all had popular small cars to offer. Renault had the R4, R5 and R6, Simca the 1000 and 1100 series; Peugeot had developed the 104, whilst Citroën began again to export its cheapest model, the 2CV, to Britain, in addition to the Dyane and the Ami. Even so, Citroën ran into difficulties in 1975.

New French models usually make their first appearance at the Paris motor show held in the autumn of each year. The first motor show in the world took place in Paris in 1898. But it

A Renault 16TX saloon car

Documentation Française

often takes six months or a year for the new models to come to Britain. Export models have to be modified. Cars for sale in Britain have to have their steering-wheel on the right. British cars for sale in France must have yellow head-lights.

French cars are popular here, but French drivers have a rather less enviable reputation, especially those from Paris and Marseilles. Despite frequent appeals on radio and TV, road accident figures are appallingly high, particularly at weekends and at holiday times.

If you drive in France you have to get used to driving on the right and overtaking on the left — you may need a passenger or a second mirror to help you to overtake if you have crossed over with your own car from Britain.

Some traffic signs and regulations will be new to you, though the main road signs have been standardised and the majority are now inter—national. Especially important is the 'priority to the right' rule. You must give way to traffic from the right at any junction where there is no sign to the contrary (passage protégé). It is very important to remember this in towns.

At a roundabout traffic circulates in an anti-clockwise direction, and cars entering the roundabout have priority over those already on it. Remember too that French road signs often point *across* the road they are indicating.

Drivers in their first year of motoring — they can hold a driving-licence from the age of 18 — must display a plastic disc on their cars to show that they must not drive faster than 90 kilometres an hour.

The 'salon de l'auto' in Paris   23

There are now speed limits on all roads in France including motorways and also stricter rules about the wearing of safety-belts. If you do speed in France, a 'motard', a motor-cycle policeman may stop you and fine you on the spot.

Finding a parking place in a town may not be too difficult as there is often 'unilateral parking', but if you park in a blue zone ('zone bleue') you must display a disc in the windscreen to show the time you arrived and the time by which you must leave.

There are all sorts of other details you must think of when you are planning a motoring holiday in France. Can you convert kilometres to miles to know how far you have to travel? Or litres to gallons to know how much petrol to buy? Or your money into francs to make sure you are being charged the right amount? And what about the language? Could you order a spare part or ask for some petrol at a garage? How about explaining to a mechanic that the car has broken down three kilometres down the road? You may need a pocket phrase-book with all the motoring terms and phrases translated. Then at least you can point to the French phrase — if you have to — but let's hope that you understand the reply!

And when you're safely on your way back, let's hope that you've not broken any customs regulations. As you arrive back in Britain and leave the car-ferry, you will see signs on the roads near the port saying 'Keep left'! and 'Tenez la gauche'! to remind returning motorists and French visitors to do just that.

Projects

1 What do the following words mean? You may see them at the roadside. route déviée, chaussée déformée, danger — verglas, poids lourds, interdit aux piétons, défense de stationner.

2 What is meant by unilateral parking? How is it organised in France?

3 What difference in the motoring laws of Britain and France have you noticed from your reading of this chapter?

4 2846 TL 13

What tells you that this car comes from the neighbourhood of Marseille?

5 Draw a diagram of an accident caused by a motorist's failure to observe the 'priorité à droite' rule.

6 You are 80 kilometres from Calais on your way home from a motoring holiday in France. Your car does 35 m.p.g. and you have just spent your last French francs on 6 litres of petrol. Will you run out of petrol before you get to the car ferry?

7 Make a list of French road signs and draw the symbols which represent them.

8 Draw on to your map the main centres of the French car industry.

9 Go to your nearest car park. Count the total number of cars and the number of French ones. Which French cars seem to be most popular?

10 Trace the journey of the French Citroën expedition through Asia. What difficulties and dangers might the expedition have faced on the way?

To discuss
Should Britain drive on the right?
Would you consider buying a French car? If so, why?

For your folder
Brochures of French cars from local agents or pictures from newspaper or magazine advertisements. The distinguishing emblems of the four French car firms, and that of Michelin. Conversion table from miles to kilometres and gallons to litres.

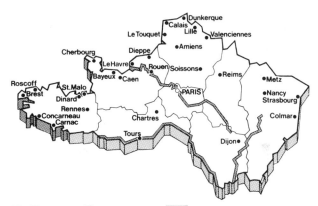

Northern France

We are now going to have a look at the towns and countryside of France, first visiting the northern half of the country which includes the Ile de France, Brittany and Normandy, the industrial north-east, and the provinces of Alsace and Lorraine on the German border.

Paris and the Ile de France

The Ile de France was one of the ancient French provinces with rivers as its boundaries and Paris as its capital.

To most Frenchmen Paris is the centre of everything: business, culture, entertainment and government. Until recently even the French navy had its headquarters in Paris.

Throughout history Paris has been a city of revolt. The French Revolution of 1789 began with the storming of the Bastille, the Paris prison. 1830 and 1848 saw further attempts at revolt by the ordinary people, who built barri-

cades across the narrow streets. Louis-Napoleon, the nephew of Napoleon Bonaparte, seeking to prevent the people of Paris rising up and barricading the streets again, appointed Baron Hausmann to redesign the city with its present circle of wide boulevards and open spaces.

Paris is sacred. In 1940, the French government could not bear the thought of the Germans bombing it. They simply moved to Tours and declared Paris an 'open city' to save it from attack. In 1944 Paris was in danger again, but fortunately the Allied armies arrived to liberate it in time and the Germans pulled out leaving its magnificent buildings intact, buildings like Notre-Dame, the Sacré-Cœur, the Louvre, the Eiffel Tower. Bye-laws ensure that public buildings are kept clean, and Paris always presents an attractive face to the tourist.

It is a city of surprises too, famous for its street markets; (flower-markets, a bird market and a flea-market), for its colonies of artists on the

Lauros

Montmartre: the Place du Tertre

hills of Montmartre and Montparnasse, for its picture galleries and museums. For a small charge you can tour the sewers of Paris, explore the catacombs by candlelight or ride up to the heights of Montmartre by funicular railway.

But the city belongs to the twentieth century too. It has a highly efficient métro system, a motorway box and enormous skyscrapers. It has its problems too: slums and shanty-towns, traffic jams, and an ever-increasing population which will perhaps reach fourteen millions by the year 2000.

Lauros

The Ile de France is Paris's larder, providing wheat from the Beauce, milk and cheese from the Brie district, fruit and vegetables from Soissons, potatoes, cattle, poultry and wine from nearby Champagne and the vineyards of Burgundy.

It also attracts tourists who flock in their thousands to visit the palaces of Versailles, Rambouillet and Fontainebleau, and cathedrals like those at Chartres and Reims.

Above: *La Défense (Paris) by night*

Normandy

To the north-west of the Ile de France lies Normandy, whose history is one of invasion. In the ninth century the Vikings colonised Normandy. It was a duke of Normandy, who invaded England in 1066 and became William the Conqueror. The story of this invasion, told from William's point of view, is illustrated in the famous Bayeux tapestry, designed and created by his queen, Matilda, and the ladies of her court.

During the Hundred Years' War the English turned the tables by invading Normandy, only to be driven out by Joan of Arc, whom they finally captured and burnt at the stake in 1431.

Finally in both World Wars, the British returned to Normandy to help drive out the Germans. It was on the coast near Cherbourg that the Allied troops landed on 'D.-Day', June 6th, 1944, to begin the liberation of France. The film, 'The Longest Day', tells how the Germans were taken completely by surprise. They were expecting an attempt further along the coast where the sea crossing is shorter.

The naval port of Cherbourg is now a terminal for the Southampton car ferry service. Le Havre also is a car ferry terminal and a port of call for ships from Europe to the United States. It is an important industrial city with its vast docks, pipe-lines and oil refineries. Caen is a centre of the steel industry. Like Le Havre, it was very largely destroyed by bombs in 1944 and has been rebuilt into a splendid modern city.

Dieppe, from a Viking word meaning 'deep', is the terminal of the Newhaven car ferry and a fishing port. At Fécamp nearby, fishermen land cod from the North Sea. The liqueur, Bénédictine, which is distilled from twenty-two different herbs, is also made there.

Ocean-going ships sail up the Seine as far as Rouen where they off-load their cargoes on to Paris-bound barges. The river frontage is lined with flour-mills, oil-refineries and chemical works.

But Normandy is not all industry — far from it! It is a land of rich dairy farms, of creamy cheeses like Camembert and Gervais, of rough cider made from the sour red apples of its extensive orchards, of the liqueur called Calvados — a sort of apple brandy — named after the département in which it is distilled. It is made at Pont-l'Evêque, which is also the home of a very well-known Normandy cheese.

To the French tourist and especially to Parisians, Normandy offers its beaches. South-west of the Seine are fashionable Deauville and Trouville

and further east in the Pays de Caux there are humbler resorts like Dieppe and Etretat, where the sea has bored tunnels into the chalk cliffs.

On the border with Brittany is Normandy's best known attraction, the Mont St-Michel, an ancient walled town high on a rock which becomes an island at high tide.

Brittany

Every summer the French pour into Brittany to enjoy fishing, sailing, bathing, skin-diving, to eat her seafoods (fruits de mer), to admire her rugged coasts and ancient towns like Quimper and St-Malo, and castles like Combourg, Josselin and Fougères. To a Frenchman a holiday here is almost as good as a holiday abroad. All around is evidence of a Celtic race: in the language which is similar to Welsh and Gaelic, and in the prehistoric stones, the dolmens and menhirs of which there are three thousand at Carnac alone.

Above: *Milk production in Normandy*
Left: *Cliffs at Etretat in Normandy*

Add to this the beauty of the calvaries in the churchyards and the processions or 'pardons' on holy days when the women wear their regional costumes and lace coiffes, and you can see why Brittany is so different from anywhere else in France.

Perhaps our tourist has already eaten early cauliflowers, potatoes, onions and artichokes from Roscoff on the north coast, or Breton lobsters and sardines from Concarneau and Douarnenez, or oysters from Cancale.

Brittany is not very industrialised. There is some shipbuilding at Brest, St-Malo and Lorient and an oil refinery at Brest. The Citroën car works are at Rennes, there is an atomic power station at Brennilis, a tidal power-station on the river Rance near Dinard, and a satellite tracking station at Lannion. There are fish canneries and a few minor industries (lighters, lenses, gloves and stockings) but no coal or steel.

Brittany always used to be one of the poorest regions in France. It was remote, cut off, an economic cul-de-sac. Too many small backward farms still exist, but many farmers have grouped themselves successfully into co-operatives to sell their market and dairy produce and buy communal equipment. But young people are still leaving the land and Brittany has to create new jobs in the towns for them. Will it succeed? If it fails, young Bretons will continue to drift away eastwards to the larger provincial towns or to Paris, or join the increasingly active separatist movement and cry "BREIZH ATAO" — "Brittany for ever"!

The north-east

Why are Alsace and Lorraine always 'lumped together'? Perhaps because they were twice seized by the Germans, in 1871 and 1940, and the teaching of French banned in their schools. Yet for the French, the two provinces have a very different image. Lorraine, with the second largest iron ore deposits in Europe, has steel-works, glass and chemical works and breweries. (Beer is more popular than wine in N.E. France.)

It is a flat region, intersected by rivers, the Meuse and the Moselle, and by canals which carry a heavy barge traffic. Metz, a grim fortress town and Nancy, famous for its beautiful Place Stanislas, together form one of the great new 'agglomérations' which will act as a counter-weight to Paris. The villages of Domremy where Joan of Arc was born, and Verdun where

Kay Lawson – Rapho

The 'pardon' at St-Yves at Tréguier in Brittany

400,000 Frenchmen died in the First World War, attract many pilgrims.

Alsace, with its pine-covered Vosges mountains, where Alsatian dogs used to defend the farms against wolves, offers the tourist spas, winter sports, lakeside resorts (Gérardmer), and lovely old towns full of half-timbered houses (Colmar). In Alsace they speak a German dialect and there are many Germanic place-names (Haguenau, Molsheim, Riquewihr).

There is some industry. Mulhouse produces textiles and potash. Strasbourg is one of Europe's great river ports. Here in 1792 Rouget de Lisle wrote the Marseillaise. And this city at the crossroads of Europe was chosen as the home for the European Parliament and the Council of Europe after the Second World War. It was to be a symbol of the new Europe, united and peaceful.

French Government Tourist Office

Guillemot

Documentation Française

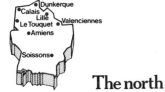

The north

To most tourists from northern Europe, the North means Calais or Boulogne (France's largest fishing-port) with their car ferry and hovercraft terminals. But few of them get to know the modest beaches of the Pas de Calais (Le Portel, Berck). They rush south in search of the sun, rather than risk an indifferent climate in northern France. Le Touquet has an international reputation and attracts many tourists to its beaches, sports events and casino. Further inland there are beautiful Gothic cathedrals at Amiens and Abbeville.

The one at Beauvais has a transept only. Its choir was so lofty that it twice collapsed, and the attempt to complete it was abandoned.

This northern region is rich in agriculture. The farms of Artois and Flanders are large and prosperous, despite the fierce battles of World War I. The main crops are wheat, potatoes, linen, barley, flax and beet. It is also a rich cattle-breeding area.

To most Frenchmen 'Le Nord' is flat, misty, damp and windy. Lorries fly along endless roads lined with poplar trees; vast barges fill the canals; its heavy industries belch out smoke.

There are textiles factories at Arras, Cambrai, Valenciennes and the huge 'agglomération' of Lille-Roubaix-Tourcoing; oil refineries and shipyards at Dunkerque; steelworks at Lille,

Denain and Dunkerque. Lens, Douai and Béthune are coal-mining areas, and there are various breweries and chemical works. All these make the north-east corner of France a part of the industrial mass of Western Europe. But its old image of miners' cottages and cobbled streets is changing fast, though some of the smaller industrial towns are still as grimly depressing as they were a century ago.

With its new motorways and the ever reviving hopes of a channel tunnel, the north looks forward to a prosperous future.

Projects

1 List the contrasts to be found between the old and the modern Paris.

2 What are 'bidonvilles'? Where and what is Sarcelles?

3 Why are poppies worn on Remembrance Day?

4 Make a list of towns with German-sounding names in Alsace and Lorraine.

5 What are menhirs and dolmens? Where in northern France can they be found in large numbers?

6 What is there at Brennilis? at Lannion? and on the river Rance near Dinard?

7 Who are the 'Johnny Onions' men?

8 What is the Council of Europe? Where are its headquarters?

9 Why are the seven burghers of Calais remembered? What famous French sculptor made a statue of them?

10 How did Baron Haussmann change the face of Paris?

11 Why are Verdun and Domremy visited by so many people?

12 Write out and learn the chorus of the Marseillaise. Why is it so called?

13 What was Operation Sealion? the Maginot Line?

14 What happened at Sedan in 1870? and at Varennes in 1791?

15 Find out all you can about these famous Bretons: Bertrand du Guesclin: Jacques Cartier: Surcouf.

16 Breton and Welsh are both Celtic languages. Look at the maps of Wales and Brittany and see if you can find any similar place names. Look particularly at the first syllables of the names.

17 Find out all you can about the Mont St-Michel, the Bayeux tapestries, Normandy cheeses.

18 Find out as much as you can about Gothic cathedrals, with photos or sketches to illustrate their characteristics.

19 Find out what you can about wine-making in Burgundy and Champagne. Draw a map showing where the main vineyards are.

20 Draw a plan of Paris and insert the following: the Ile de la Cité, Montmartre, the Louvre, the Latin Quarter, Montparnasse, the Bois de Boulogne.

21 What are the main differences between Alsace and Lorraine?

22 Find out all you can about farming in northern France.

23 Find out what you can about industry in northern France.

24 Find out what you can about Breton 'pardons', regional costumes and customs.

To discuss
Should there be a channel tunnel?

For your folder
Pictures from travel brochures, travel articles, postcards.

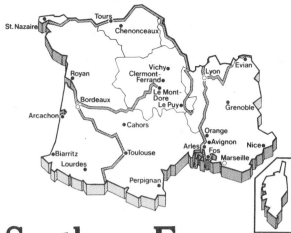

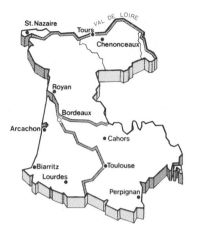

Southern France

South-west France

The river Loire is almost a natural dividing line between north and south on the western side of France. Along its banks stand castles like Chambord, Chenonceaux and Blois, telling of royal and aristocratic luxury in the 16th and 17th centuries; and fortress castles like Loches and Angers with their keeps and dungeons, recalling the grimmer realities of medieval times.

Crossing the Loire in a southerly direction is almost like crossing into another country, where the climate is warmer, the vegetation more lush and the people more Mediterranean in temperament and outlook.

Roger Perrin – Atlas

This region of France, stretching along the Atlantic seaboard from the Loire to the Pyrenees and over to the western end of France's Mediterranean coast, is a haven for holiday-makers.

Its chief beaches are Royan, Arcachon and Biarritz (a favourite haunt of King Edward VII) on the Atlantic coast, and Collioure and a string of new resorts on the Languedoc coast where, between Montpellier and Perpignan, six completely new holiday complexes have been built on what used to be 120 miles of mosquito-ridden marshes. La Grande Motte is typical of these. Fewer Frenchmen will want, it is hoped, to spend their holidays in Spain.

Lauros – Beaugard

Above: *La Grande Motte*
Left: *Chenonceaux*

31

Jean Dieuzaide

Winter sports at Superbagnères

In fact much of the south-west is known for its food and drink: Cognac for its brandy, Périgord for its truffles and 'pâté de foie gras' and Agen for its sun-dried prunes. The Lot-et-Garonne has peach and apple orchards, oysters come from Arcachon and Marennes, and fish from La Rochelle and Saint-Jean-de-Luz. Most of the Languedoc too is now fertile thanks to irrigation from the Rhône canals.

South of Bordeaux vast forests were planted to reclaim marshland along the Atlantic coast. Now the pine trees are tapped for their resin, and timber and cellophane products are important resources of the region.

A little further west you can ski in the Pyrenees or go to spas like Cauterets and Luchon. The Pyrenees with their Basque and Catalan enclaves, have the appeal of a foreign land, as also does the tiny little state of Andorra perched up in the mountains.

Every year hundreds of thousands of helpless invalids go in special hospital trains to Lourdes, seeking a miracle cure in the waters of the grotto where Bernadette saw her visions in the last century.

Two important discoveries were made in the south-west: at Les Eyzies in the Dordogne the bones of a Cromagnon man, perhaps 50,000 years old, were found; and at Lascaux there are cave-paintings of animals by prehistoric man. The caves were discovered quite by chance in 1940 when four boys, out playing with their dog, followed it when it disappeared down a hole and found themselves in the famous 'grottes'.

The area round Bordeaux is famous for its wine. As early as 1307 it sent a thousand casks of claret to Britain for the coronation of Edward II.

There is not a great deal of industry in this region, but what there is, is spectacular. In 1954 the French struck oil at Parentis; also in the fifties, drillings at Lacq led to the discovery of very high-pressure natural gas. A brand new city of 12,000 people had to be built near Lacq to house the workers from the industries which sprang up.

At St-Nazaire the luxury liner 'France' was built. Toulouse makes aircraft. Concorde 001 made its maiden flight from Toulouse in March 1969. The city also houses a space centre which launches, tracks and recovers rockets.

French Government Tourist Office (Ph. Yan)

Natural gas plant at Lacq in the Pyrenees

The Massif Central

This vast granite plateau right in the heart of France is covered with dense forests interspersed with pastureland and lakes and characterised by its 'puys', the conical-shaped cores of extinct volcanoes. Rivers run down from it in all directions and the fast flowing Dordogne in particular has a series of hydro-electric power stations.

The tourist may 'take a cure' at a spa, such as Vichy, la Bourboule, le Mont-Dore or Royat. He may visit an 11th century 'romanesque' cathedral (one with rounded arches) at Le Puy, Conques, St-Nectaire; or the great fortress cathedral at Albi. He may think of the stormy history of the old province of the Auvergne as he looks at the many ruined castles. He may go ski-ing on the slopes of the Puy de Sancy.

His car tyres probably come from the Michelin works at Clermont-Ferrand. Perhaps he has some porcelain from Limoges or even a piece of tapestry from Aubusson. He may wear gloves from Millau, use an umbrella from Aurillac or knives from Thiers.

He knows all about the cheeses of the Cantal and St-Nectaire, and Roquefort (a blue-veined cheese matured in underground caves from the milk of a million ewes) is a special luxury and perhaps the king of French cheeses. The Charolais cattle which graze on the mountains provide meat as well as breeding-stock for export. Sheep too are reared in their thousands on the Causses, the limestone uplands in the Lot, and brought down to the plains in winter.

Apart from some coal at St-Etienne and Decazeville there are hardly any raw materials. Farms are small and peasants are leaving for the towns in large numbers. The Massif Central may one day become a vast national park or nature reserve.

Karquel   French Government Tourist Office

Michelin

Church of St-Michael d'Aiguilhe on its hilltop at Le Puy

Michelin's test circuit near Clermont-Ferrand

The south-east and Corsica

The great loop of the Rhône, as it flows from Switzerland towards its delta, encloses Provence and the French Alps, a Mecca for tourists of every nation.

There are winter sports in the Savoy Alps. Mont Blanc (4,807m) is the highest mountain in Europe. You can climb mountains the hard way or go up by téléphérique. Lakeside spas (Evian, Aix-les-Bains) are strictly for the well-off. There are Roman cities: Orange with its theatre and triumphal arch; Arles, where gladiators have given way to bull-fighters in the ancient arena; Nîmes, whose Maison Carrée is an old Roman temple, though it is not, as its name would imply, square; and the Pont du Gard, the aqueduct that brought fresh water fifty kilometres into Nîmes.

There is Avignon with its twelfth century bridge and the papal palace where seven popes lived in luxury in the fourteenth century, and there are the famous Mediterranean resorts of Nice, Cannes, St-Tropez and Monte-Carlo.

The South-east provides food and drink for the French table: wine, olive oil, garlic, fruit and vegetables. The marshes of the Camargue have been drained and turned into rice-fields and the famous black bulls provide both meat and the local, non-bloody, form of bull-fighting.

French Government Tourist Office

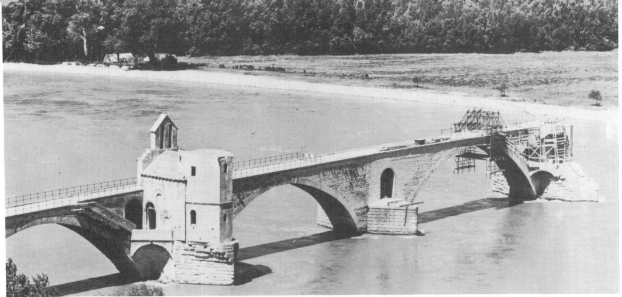

Flowers, chiefly for the perfume factories of Grasse, are a valuable product. On average three new perfumes are launched each year and each new perfume can take from three to five years to perfect.

Corsica sends milk to the mainland to be made into cheese. Goats and sheep graze in the 'maquis', a sort of stunted forest which gave its name to the French Resistance Army in the Second World War.

To the old industries — silk and textiles for which Lyon has long been renowned, and the processing of colonial goods such as sugar,

cocoa, palm oil, and coffee at Marseille — we must add the new ones helped by the electricity from the Rhône barrages. One of these is the mining and processing of the great deposits of aluminium near Brignoles.

West of Marseille the coast is studded with oil refineries, notably those of the Etang de Berre and Lavéra. Huge modern oil tankers are built at La Ciotat and La Seyne and can now dock at the new port of Fos, the first port in Europe capable of taking ships of over 200,000 tons. France's atomic missiles are stored in underground silos near Apt. Grenoble makes apparatus for hydro electric and atomic power stations and is perhaps the fastest growing city in France. Its population has increased fourfold since 1945.

The South–east now hums with industrial activity. One day the Rhône will be as busy a commercial waterway as the Rhine, and a Rhône-Rhine canal may link the Mediterranean to the North Sea.

Opposite page: *The Pont du Gard near Nîmes*
Top: *Twelfth-century bridge at Avignon*
Left: *Petrol tanker at the new port of Fos*

Projects

1 Where and what are the Landes?

2 List some of the differences between northern and southern France.

3 Name the most popular beaches along the Atlantic and Mediterranean coasts.

4 What evidences of Roman France can still be seen in the south?

5 What is made at the following places: Grasse? Brignoles? Roquefort?

6 What important industry is carried on at St-Nazaire?

7 Why do so many pilgrims go to Lourdes?

8 Why are there so many barrages on the river Dordogne?

9 Which is the odd man out? Lancôme, Coty, Eau de Cologne, Chanel.

10 Match these:– Princess Grace, Brigitte Bardot, the Promenade des Anglais, the International Film Festival, to the following towns: Nice, Cannes, St-Tropez, Monte-Carlo.

11 Find out what happened at Toulon in 1793 and 1942: on the Vercors plateau in 1944: Orange in 1673 and Avignon in 1791.

12 Find out what you can about the mistral: bauxite: the Camargue: Van Gogh at Arles: the bridge at Avignon: the Rhône barrages.

13 Draw a map of the Bordeaux wine area. What scandal in 1974 harmed Bordeaux's reputation? Which is the odd man out? Sauternes, Médoc, Graves, Champagne, St-Emilion.

14 Find out what happened at La Rochelle in 1628: at Roncevalles in 778: at St-Nazaire in 1943.

15 Draw a map showing the industrial importance of south and south-west France.

16 Find out all you can about the food and drink produced in southern France.

17 Draw a map showing the Châteaux of the Loire valley. What two main types of castle are there? Which is the odd man out? Blois, Rambouillet, Azay-le-Rideau, Chambord, Loches.

18 Find out as much as you can about the traces of prehistoric man in the south-west of France.

19 Find out what you can about 'romanesque' churches. How do they differ from Gothic ones?

To discuss
The value of 'son et lumière' spectacles to attract tourists to an area.

For your folder
Collect pictures, post cards etc. of the following:
Castles, romanesque churches and cathedrals, Roman monuments, prehistoric remains.
File travel articles from newspapers or magazines and mark in on your map the places they mention.

Railways

Until shortly before the Second World War, French railways were almost a standing joke. Engines billowed forth smoke and steam, showers of sparks endangered nearby crops. Trains were ugly and dirty, and seldom ran to time. They still had third class carriages with slatted wooden seats which must have been among the first ever built and journeys in them were sheer torture.

Today France has one of the most modern and efficient railway systems in the world. How was this transformation possible in such a relatively short space of time?

The smashing of the main railway network by allied bombers in 1944 in order to stop German troop movements was one of the main reasons for this rapid modernisation. The destruction was so great that a vast re-building programme was embarked upon immediately after the war.

Steam gave way to diesel and electricity, and by 1964 there were about 10,000 kilometres of electrified line. France was producing some of the fastest trains in the world. For example, the 'turbotrain' – a 'jet-engined' express – reached a top speed of 307 kilometres an hour on a test run. More revolutionary still is the aérotrain, invented by Jean Bertin. It works on the same principle as the hovercraft (aéroglisseur) and is driven by propellers like an aeroplane. Jets of air lift it just above its concrete track and the complete absence of any friction makes very high speeds possible. The first trains are due to run between Paris and Orléans and will travel at 300 km per hour. It is hoped that one day it may

link Paris with her outer suburbs and nearby towns and provide an ultra-rapid commuter service.

Documentation Française

French Railways Y. Bronchard   Société de l'aérotrain (Jean Bertin)

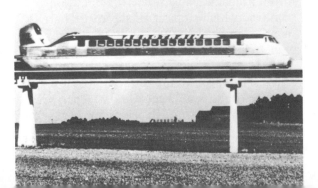

Top: *Destruction of the railways in '44*
Middle: *Diesel/electric locomotive*
Bottom: *Jean Bertin's 'aérotrain'*

Another 'super' train service is the T.E.E. (Trans-Europa-Express) which links French cities to other European centres. Each country – Holland, Belgium, Germany, Switzerland, Spain, Italy – designs its own train. Some have diesel locomotives, others electric. All have a red and white T.E.E. on the front of the engine. The T.E.E. travels very fast (200 k.p.h.) It is air-conditioned and sound-proof. On it you can have the services of a secretary or a hairdresser. You can phone your office in Paris or Brussels. But naturally a T.E.E. trip is very expensive: you have to pay a supplement on top of the first-class fare.

Here are the names of some of these trains.

Brabant *(Paris – Brussels)*
Cisalpin *(Paris – Milan)*
Edelweiss *(Amsterdam – Zurich)*
Goethe *(Paris – Frankfurt)*
Ile-de-France *(Paris – Amsterdam)*
Mont-Cenis *(Lyon – Milan)*
Parsifal *(Paris – Hamburg)*
Aquitaine *(Paris – Bordeaux)*
Mistral *(Paris – Nice)*
Kleber *(Paris – Strasbourg)*
Stanislas *(Paris – Strasbourg)*

On the more mundane every-day passenger services you have the choice of travelling by the 'rapide' which is extremely fast, has very few stops, but usually involves a supplement over and above the normal fare, the 'express' which stops at most sizeable towns, or the 'train-omnibus' which stops at all stations. There is also the 'autorail', a two-car diesel serving branch lines.

There is a 'wagon-restaurant' on most long-distance trains, and 'wagon-lits' (sleepers) if the train is travelling through the night. If you can't

Documentation Française

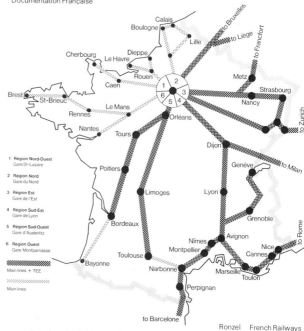

Ronzel   French Railways

Top: *A T.E.E. train*
Middle: *Map of railway network*
Bottom: *Breakfast is served in a wagon-lit*

afford a meal in the dining-car, you can buy rolls and drinks from a trolley which is wheeled up and down the corridor and there are refreshment trolleys on the platform at many of the larger stations too.

Opposite is a map of the French railway system, showing how the main lines all radiate from Paris with its six big termini, each of which serves a different region of France.

The main drawback to such a centralised system is that, whereas you can easily get to Paris from anywhere in the country, cross-country journeys are tediously slow. Competition from road transport has closed many branch lines, and the use of pipelines for the transport of oil has meant a further loss to the railways.

Here finally are a few figures.

The French railway system is the third longest in the world after those of the U.S.S.R. and the U.S.A.

Over 80% of main lines are electrified.

The 'Capitole' (Paris – Toulouse) is the fastest train in Europe. It once reached 331 kilometres an hour on a stretch of line near Bordeaux.

Before we leave the subject of trains let us have a brief look at the

Paris métro

The Paris Métro dates from 1900 when the first line was opened. Nowadays more than four million passengers use it every day. The trains, 'les rames', run just below ground level and follow the direction of the streets and boule-vards, travelling fairly slowly and stopping frequently.

There is a Métro map at the entrance to each station and the lines are usually referred to by the names of their first and last stations: i.e. Vincennes – Neuilly, Dauphine – Nation and so on.

You may have to change at a 'station de correspondance', a station which serves two or more lines. A diagram in the carriage will tell you which line to change to, and an orange sign above the exit from the platform marked 'correspondance' will show you which way you must go.

There is an abundance of clearly marked direction signs like the ones illustrated below, so that even the least experienced traveller can have little difficulty in finding his way around. There is one first-class carriage in the middle of the train and a sign on the platform showing where it will pull up. You pay the same fare whether you travel for two stops or go round and round underground all day! To save money you can buy a 'carnet' of ten tickets which works out cheaper.

Fernand Marty

In the Paris Métro

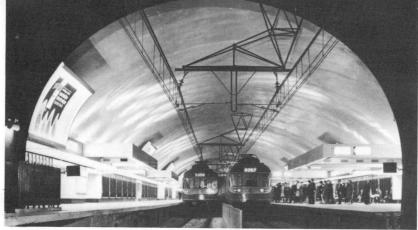

R.A.T.P.

The R.A.T.P. (Régie Autonome des Transports Parisiens) has started a big programme of modernisation and the Métro is becoming more and more automatic. Ticket-collectors are rapidly disappearing. The newest trains have no driver, though the guard has a manual control in case anything goes wrong. New trains have rubber tyres to cut down noise, and moving corridors, 'trottoirs roulants', are being installed where changing trains would entail a particularly long walk.

In 1969 the first section of a regional express network (the R.E.R.) 'Réseau Express Régional' was inaugurated to provide a quicker link between Paris and the outer suburbs. Its new terminal, where absolutely everything is automatic, is like something out of a science fiction novel.

Projects

1 What are the differences between a rapide, an express and a train-omnibus?

2 Why are the following Métro stations so called? Stalingrad, Pasteur, Bastille, Austerlitz, Franklin D. Roosevelt.

3 On the Métro, how would you go from Trocadéro to Châtelet? from the Gare de l'Est to Madeleine? from Stalingrad to the Gare de Lyon?

4 You arrive in France in Calais and want to get to Rouen. What is the quickest way of getting there by train?

5 You want to tour the French Riviera by car. Compare the advantages of a)motor rail, b)rail and car hire, c)fly and car hire.

6 On your map of France copy the main railway lines from the diagram on page 38. Put in the names of the chief towns.

7 Say why the eleven T.E.E. trains are so named.

8 Draw (or paste in) a copy of the Métro map. List the stations which serve an interesting place or monument. Find out all you can about these places.

9 What are the six Paris rail termini called? What towns do they lead to?

10 Try to trace the history of the French railways from their beginnings in 1825.

To discuss
The disadvantages of a centralised railway system.

For your folder
Rail and métro tickets, pages from time-tables, pictures of trains and stations, maps showing rail network. A copy of the métro map.

Entertainment

How French teenagers spend their leisure time depends very much on where they live. Paris is different from the rest of France, and life in the country is very different from life in the big cities. In fact life in the provinces can sometimes be very dull for a teenager.

An early start to the working day means that people tend to go to bed early. A long working day means that they arrive home late in the evening, and the shortened evening is sometimes taken up entirely by the evening meal — a family occasion when the whole family sits round the table talking.

The weekly dance or disco on a Saturday night is probably the highlight of the week for many teenagers in rural France. Most small towns have an annual fair or 'fête'. In addition there is national holiday on the 14th of July, when firework displays all over the country celebrate the storming of the Bastille and the foundation of the French republic.

Pop-music is as popular in France as elsewhere and most towns have discothèques, but most of the actual pop-music is imported from America or Britain. French pop-singers often make records in English, hoping to sell more this way, but in fact few French pop-singers are known in Britain and America although some singers and groups adopt English names. For instance, Johnny Halliday's real name is Jean-Philippe Smet, and his style of singing, along with that of his wife, Sylvie Vartan, and artistes like Mireille Mathieu, Sheila and Adamo are far more popular in France than American-style pop-music. Also very popular are the clever, witty songs written and sung by contemporary song-writers like Jacques Brel, Georges Brassens and Moustaki. Most French teenagers own a transistor radio, and listen regularly to stations like Europe numéro 1 and Radio Luxembourg which give them popular music of one kind or another all day long.

Many magazines like 'Salut les Copains' and 'Mademoiselle Age Tendre' are written for the 13 to 16 year-old age group. They have articles on pop-stars and the hit-parade, horoscopes, fashion hints and problem pages (courrier du cœur), and large pull-out coloured photos of favourite singers and movie stars.

41

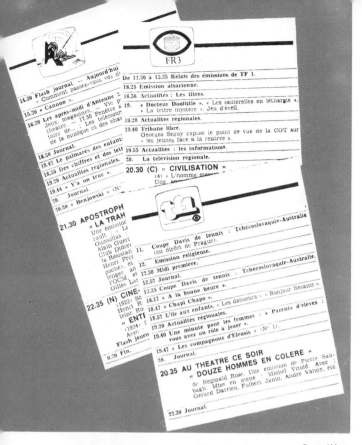

Top: *Some television programmes*
Bottom: *A Paris café*

If a teenager stays at home in the evening there is of course television. There are three channels, referred to as TF1, A2 and FR3. (Télévision de France, Antenne 2, France Régions.) These are now independently run, though they are still answerable to the government for the content of their programmes. You can find details of them in a weekly magazine called 'Télé 7 Jours', and of course in the newspapers.

Can you recognise any of their programmes? Here are a few which you will surely know: le Virginien, Le Manège Enchanté, Barbapapa, L'homme de Fer, les Six Femmes de Henri VIII, Jeux sans Frontières.
Eurovision broadcasts are shown all over Europe and cover sport and events like the popular Eurovision Song Contest.

Not all French homes by any means have television even today, and many of those who have no set of their own watch T.V. at their local café, which, particularly in the country, is often the centre of the community. Here you can meet your friends over a drink of wine or coffee — or Coca-cola — play dominoes or cards, or simply sit outside at a pavement table and watch the world go by. Often there is a selection of daily papers provided for customers. Cafés are open to everyone, but no alcoholic drinks are served to anyone under eighteen. Some have juke-boxes and pin-tables with games like 'le baby-foot' (table football).

French teenagers often complain about their lack of freedom. They are tied to their family unit more than the British teenager. The different meanings of the word 'parent' in French and English perhaps highlight this point. In French the word includes grandparents and great-grandparents, aunts and uncles, nephews and nieces, and cousins however distant — anyone in fact who belongs to the family. And this family unit has a grand reunion as often as possible — at weddings and christenings, at Christmas and birthdays. French Catholics tend to celebrate their saint's day as well as their birthday, and every day in the year bears the name of its own particular saint.

Young British workers and students often become independent by living away from home. Girls often share flats, for example. This is much less frequently done in France. Teenage girls are not really supposed to go out alone in the evenings, to a dance for example. They go out in groups, often on mopeds. These are very popular as you do not have to have a licence in order to ride one. If teenagers stay at home, they sometimes arrange 'une boum', an informal party for their friends who come along armed with their favourite records for an evening of music and dancing.

Small wonder that French teenagers are sometimes envious of their British and American counterparts and mischievously refer to the older generation as 'les vieux' or, even more unkindly, as 'les croulants'.

The French government is making an effort to provide more leisure opportunities for the younger generation. Nowadays there are 'Maisons des Jeunes' in nearly all towns, often really enterprising youth clubs for the under — eighteens. They pay a membership fee to join and can then take part in various activities, sports like judo or basket-ball, hobbies like pottery or woodwork. There are also film shows, plays and illustrated talks, and a full-scale programme all day on Wednesdays when the schools are closed.

Fernand Marty

Sappa

Top: *Greetings cards*
Middle: *Teenagers on their mopeds*
Bottom: *'Maison des Jeunes' in Paris*

43

In major towns there are 'Maisons de la Culture' which cater especially for the eighteen to twenty-one age group. They specialise in the arts, not only presenting live performances by orchestras, ballet and theatre companies, but encouraging young people to develop their own talents in drama, in music, in painting and so on.

The French cinema has an international reputation. Small cinemas still exist in the surburbs of towns, as well as the larger town-centre cinemas. Some films are for adults only ('interdit aux moins de 18 ans'). The cashier can check on the age of any teenagers by asking to see their identity cards. Everyone has to carry a 'carte d'identité'. The Catholic church acts as

Pierre Cry   Documentation Française

Documentation Française

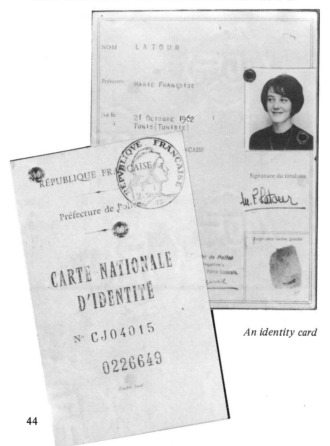

An identity card

Top: *'Maison de la Culture' at Amiens*
Middle: *The library of the 'Maison de la Culture'*
          at Reims
Bottom: *Poster of an American film*

44

an unofficial censor: it recommends some films, does not recommend others and denounces some as quite undesirable. Smoking in cinemas is not allowed, but there is an interval when people can go out and smoke in the foyer. Usually there are separate performances, as in the theatre, so you do not have to keep getting up from your seat to let late-comers pass, nor on the other hand can you stay to see the film through twice! Normally there is only one feature film and the rest of the programme is made up of advertisements, a short cartoon or a documentary and a trailer. Many British and American films are shown in France. Some have the original sound-track with French sub-titles (v.o. version originale), some have the sound-track dubbed in French (v.f. version française).

Though Paris is the real centre of the theatre and the home of famous companies like the Comédie Francaise, most of the main provincial towns have a theatre. Rennes and Rouen have excellent repertory companies. At the international drama festival held in Avignon each summer, the accent is on youth and drama students and young people can work together and exchange ideas.

Perhaps after all then, French teenagers are not so very unfortunate wherever they may live. Entertainment and leisure activities have been provided for them in towns and villages throughout the country, and Paris is no longer the only centre of cultural life as it was twenty or thirty years ago.

Projects

1   Why is it not easy for a French teenager to get into a cinema where an X-film is being shown?

2   Fit English names to these T.V. programmes: le Virginien, le Manège Enchanté, l'Homme de Fer, Jeux sans Frontières. Are any of these original French programmes?

3   List and draw the following means of transport popular with young French people:
le vélo, le vélomoteur, le scooter, la moto.

4   Make a list of the sports and activities you would expect to find at a 'Maison des Jeunes et de la Culture'.

5   Make or adapt a calendar for the present year. Mark in the following national holidays: Noël, le jour de l'an, lundi de Pâques, lundi de Pentecôte, l'Assomption, la Toussaint, la Fête Nationale, la Fête du Travail, l'Armistice (1918).

6   Find as many French language stations as you can on your radio set. Make a list of their names and wave-lengths and the times of any regular programmes you can recognise.

To Discuss
Would you prefer to be a French teenager?
What do you think of compulsory identity cards?

For your folder
Extracts from French teenage magazines.
Photographs of pop-stars and groups.
A collage from 'Télé-7-Jours' showing the three channels. List items of interest from each.
Photographs of French film stars and stills from their films.
Horoscopes and 'Courrier du Cœur' from magazines.

Other means of transport

Roads

France has large stretches of flat country. It has the most extensive network of roads of any country in the world. The Romans made four thousand kilometres of good military roads. France's roads then fell into decay, but by the end of the 18th century, the present system of tree-lined roads was taking shape. Napoleon was a great roadbuilder, mainly for military reasons. As with the railway system, most main roads converge on Paris.

Upkeep of main roads is in the hands of a central state organisation called the 'Ponts et Chaussées' (literally 'bridges and highways'). These are the 'N' roads, the 'routes nationales'. Each 'département' is responsible for its own 'routes départementales' or 'D' roads, and each 'commune' for the 'routes vicinales' or 'V' roads.

Until comparatively recently there were few 'autoroutes' (motorways) or even 'routes à chaussées séparées' (dual-carriageways), but recent development has been rapid and France now has a growing network of 'A' roads. There is continuous motorway from Lille and Rouen in the north right down to Marseille and the Côte d'Azur. Paris has her 'boulevard périphérique' (motorway ring road) with exit points for 'A' roads to Chartres, Orléans and the ever-growing ring of new towns on the fringe of the capital.

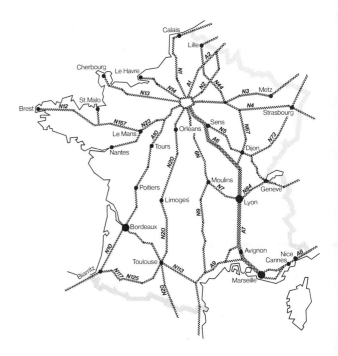

46

French Government Tourist Office

S. R. I. P.

Fast, heavy lorries, 'poids lourds', and petrol tankers carry far less merchandise than the railways. Lorries carrying fruit, meat and fish are often refrigerated.

Two spectacular feats of civil engineering in recent years are the Tancarville bridge over the Seine, linking Le Havre with western France, and the Mont Blanc tunnel, jointly built by French and Italian labour at a cost of 265 francs per centimetre. Unlike the mountain passes, it is open throughout the year — a boon to both tourism and trade.

Air travel

France has a proud aerial history. The Mont-golfier brothers flew the first ballon in 1783. Blériot was the first to fly the Channel in 1909. Mermoz opened up a postal service in 1930 from France to Buenos Aires and over the Andes into Chile. In the same year Costes flew non-stop from Paris to New York.

Every year French airlines fly nearly four times the distance between the earth and the moon. Air-France, mainly state-owned, has one of the world's largest networks. It serves seventy-four countries.

Internal services are run by Air-Inter. It links Paris with about thirty towns throughout France. There are also flights from Lyon to a number of large provincial towns, and some intercity helicopters.

Paris has three airports, Orly, Le Bourget, and the newest one at Roissy, which has been built to take supersonic aircraft like Concorde. Nice is France's second biggest airport for traffic, and Marseille the third. There is also a night postal

Top: *The bridge at Tancarville*
Bottom: *Motorway interchange near Paris*

service linking Paris to the main cities. A letter posted in Lille at 8 p.m. is on the breakfast table on the Côte d'Azur the following morning.

Owing to the repeated German invasions of northern France, large parts of the aircraft industry were based on Toulouse. Here, at the Sud-Aviation works, Caravelles (first flights 1959) and Concordes (manufactured jointly with B.A.C. Bristol) are produced. The French also build fighters like the Mirage and Breguet, part of the European air-bus, as well as rockets, missiles and satellites (for communications and weather forecasts).

Documentation Française (Aérospatiale)

Waterways

France has never fully exploited the possibilities of her waterways as her neighbours in northern Europe have done.

It is true that canals were built in the 17th and 18th centuries: for example, the Briare canal linking the Loire with the Seine, and the Canal du Midi linking the Garonne with the Mediterranean, but these carry little commercial traffic.

Of her rivers only the Seine and the Oise are fully used. Paris, though it is more than 200 kilometres from the sea is France's largest port after Marseille and Le Havre.

Most traffic is in the north, where broad canals and huge barges link the industrial towns of the north-east with Belgium and Germany, and the Seine links Paris with the Atlantic. Ocean-going vessels can come down the Seine and trans-ship goods at Rouen into barges for Paris. They carry raw materials like coal and iron ore, as well as building materials, fertilisers, petroleum products. Renault cars made in Paris for export

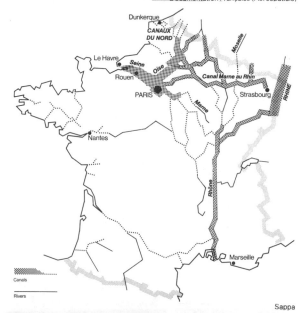

Sappa

Top: *Airbus, Caravelle and Concorde at Toulouse*
Middle: *Map of canal network*
Bottom: *A 'pusher' tug*

travel down the Seine as far as Rouen where they are trans-shipped to ocean-going or cross-channel freighters.

In the south of France stretches of the Rhône have been canalised to by-pass parts where the current is too strong for navigation, and in the not too distant future there may well be broad waterways linking the Rhine with the Seine and the Atlantic, and Marseille with Germany and the North Sea. Some canals, like the one linking the Rhône at Arles to Narbonne, are for irrigation.

Finally, canals are popular with tourists. Every year there is a race across Brittany from St-Malo to the Atlantic, and a tourist who is not in a hurry could go through France by boat from the Channel right down to the Mediterranean.

Projects

1 What is the name of the new airport at Roissy near Paris?

2 Find out more about Blériot, St-Exupéry and Mermoz.

3 Which of these aircraft is not built at Toulouse? Caravelle, Concorde, A300B Airbus, Jaguar, Mirage, Harrier.

4 Draw a diagram of France's internal air routes.

5 On your map of France reproduce the skeleton road map and insert the principal towns.

6 What part did the small town of Mazamet play in road safety propaganda?

7 Draw the road signs for each of the following: chaussée déformée, sens unique, passage protégé, interdiction d'avertisseur, route nationale, stationnement interdit.

8 Using a good road map of France, plan the following journeys so as to by-pass Paris.
a) Rennes to Reims, b) Boulogne to Dijon, c) Tours to Lille.

9 Which way would you go if you were taking: –
a a consignment of fish from Concarneau (Brittany) to Lyon?
b a load of fruit from Cavaillon (Provence) to Metz (Lorraine)?

10 Plan a journey through France by boat from Le Havre to Nice. Show by diagrams what waterways you would use and what places you would pass through. Illustrate where possible with pictures of the country you would cross.

11 On your map of France trace the following waterways: –
a Bordeaux – Toulouse – Sète
b St-Malo to the Atlantic
c The Marne-Rhine canal linking Paris and Strasbourg

To discuss
The advantages and disadvantages of supersonic aircraft like Concorde.
Are canals worth building? Mention some of the difficulties of constructing them.

For your folder
Any pictures concerned with roads: a bus time-table, a road licence, an Auto-Ecole car, a long-distance lorry, a newspaper cutting describing an accident in France, a map of the main road system.
Pictures of as many French planes as you can find.
Air time-tables, both Air France and Air Inter.
Pictures of barges on inland waterways, river ports, pusher tugs, barge lifts to avoid locks.

Government

The Assemblée Nationale

Fernand Marty

The Frenchman resents authority. He despises a weak government, but if there is a strong one, he wants to overthrow it.

Who exactly governs France? First, there is the central government in Paris. Then there is local government in town and country. Both have civil servants (fonctionnaires) and police (agents and gendarmes) to carry out their decisions.

The national government

In 1793 the French royal family — Louis XVI and his queen Marie-Antoinette were beheaded on the guillotine. Yet almost another eighty years passed before a republic was finally established. In 1870 the disastrous defeat of the French by the Prussians, the siege of Paris and the loss of the provinces of Alsace and Lorraine brought the Empire to an end and the Third Republic into being.

The Republican motto is 'Liberté, Egalité, Fraternité' and all public buildings, ministries, hospitals, law-courts, schools, carry these words over their doorways or on their façades.

France has always been a difficult country to govern. When de Gaulle came to power in 1958, he was determined to end the weak government which France had suffered since the end of the Second World War in particular. In those thirteen years France had had a series of rapidly changing Prime Ministers. On average there was a new government (though not new elections) every six months. Ministers constantly changed or lost their jobs. Political parties joined together to form coalitions. But these kept breaking up because the parties couldn't agree. 'Government defeat!' the headlines in the papers cried.

De Gaulle created a new constitution for the Fifth Republic. It gave more power to the President and less to Parliament. This is how it works.

Every seven years, all French men and women over the age of 18 can vote for a President. Every five years, they send 488 members (députés) to the French parliament (L'Assemblée).

There is also an upper house, the Senate, with 316 members (Sénateurs), but it has little power.

After the election, the President picks his Prime Minister who is usually the leader of the largest political party. (There are at least twenty parties in France.) With the Prime Minister's help, the President chooses his cabinet ministers who include the Home Secretary (Ministre de l'Intérieur), Foreign Secretary (Ministre des Affaires Etrangères) and about fourteen others. The Prime Minister in France is much less important than his opposite number in England, for example. The French President is not only the head of state, but head of the government as well.

Today in the Fifth Republic, the President with his Cabinet is much stronger than the Assembly. By law, the President can dismiss the Assembly and order fresh elections if it keeps blocking the laws he and his Cabinet wish to push through.

Budgets are important, for they provide the government with the money it needs. If the Assembly spends more than ten weeks discussing the budget, the President can get it through by special order.

The President can by-pass parliament and ask the people themselves for their opinion ('Oui' or 'Non') on a particular issue. This is called a referendum. De Gaulle used the referendum on more than one occasion. At the time of the Algerian insurrection, for example, a big 'Oui' from the people gave de Gaulle a vote of confidence so that he was able to act independently of parliament.

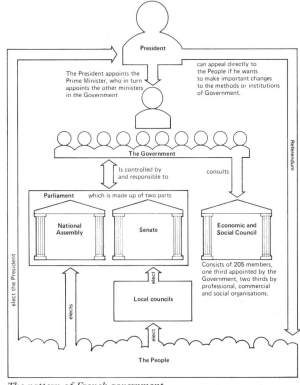

The pattern of French government

This constitution did exactly what de Gaulle hoped it would. It gave France a firm government based on a strong President.

But in 1968 there was an attempt at revolution, led mainly by students noisily demanding reforms. Again de Gaulle went to the people, but in the 1971 referendum the nation for the first time said 'Non' to him. He at once resigned and left political life for good.

Sappa

The civil service

The Civil Service puts into effect the decisions of the President and his Cabinet. For example, if the government decided to raise the school-leaving age to seventeen (it is actually sixteen), the civil servants in the Ministry of Education with the help of the 'académies' (see page 13) and of the teachers who are also civil servants, would see that this was done.

Local government

Everything in France is directed from Paris. Everything is centralised. What Paris says, goes. Paris is like an octopus with tentacles reaching out all over the country.

In each of the 95 French 'départements' (counties) the State appoints its own governor. He is called a 'préfet' (prefect). The départements were made small in the first place so that the prefect could travel by carriage from his seat in the county town to the border of his county and back within twenty-four hours. In each sub-division of the county (arrondissement) there is a sub-prefect. Finally, each arrondissement is divided into the smallest units of all, the 'communes'.

Each commune has a mayor. Everyone over 18 living in one of the 38,000 communes can vote to elect a local council. This happens every six years. The councillors who are elected then choose the mayor. Some mayors stay in office a very long time. A commune in Normandy recently had a mayor who was ninety, and blind.

The mayor chooses his assistants (adjoints), who deputise for him if he is absent or ill.

The council has from eleven to thirty-seven members, depending on the size of the commune. It must meet at least four times a year.

What are the duties of the mayor?

He must register all births, marriages and deaths in the commune.

The mayor officiates at marriages. You are not legally married in France until you have been to the council offices or Town Hall (Hôtel de Ville), where the mayor, wearing his red, white and blue sash, performs a simple ceremony and signs the register. If you wish to be married in church, the religious service takes place afterwards.

The mayor is responsible for maintaining law and order. He calls in the police when necessary. On his notice-board outside the 'mairie' he publishes official notices, including for example, the date when the young men of the commune have to report for their military service.

He welcomes important visitors to the commune. He may kick off at an important football match, and he even has a duty to bury down-and-outs free of charge in the local cemetery!

Documentation Française (Almasy)

The mayor officiating at a wedding

Gendarmerie Nationale

In actual fact, the mayor is the representative of the government in the commune, rather than its head. He is very much under the thumb of the sub-prefect — over what he puts into his budget, for example. He may have to ask the sub-prefect for a grant if he cannot collect enough money from local taxes and rates. The 'préfet' can suspend or even dismiss him. This happened some years ago to a mayor in a village in Normandy, who let an old building for a wedding reception. The floor was rotten and some of the wedding guests fell through it into an ancient well underneath the building and were drowned. The mayor, either from remorse, or because of the disgrace of his dismissal, later committed suicide.

So as to be more efficient, the départements are now being grouped into twenty-two regions. These correspond to the old provinces of Brittany, Burgundy, Auvergne and so on, and each of these larger regions has a 'super'-prefect.

There is also a move towards decentralisation in France by creating new provincial capitals which will take over much of the authority so far wielded by Paris.

The police

The French are 'against' authority — and particularly therefore against those watchdogs of authority, the police. Since France is not exactly a law-abiding country and is sometimes a violent one, the police are very numerous and always armed.

The nearest the French have to a 'village bobby' is the 'garde-champêtre' in the small commune. He arrives, notebook in hand, if for example a careless shopkeeper has left litter on the pavement.

Above: *Police questioning a motorist*
Top: *Map showing the twenty-two regions*

53

In the larger communes of over ten thousand people, police duties are carried out by 'agents de police'. As for the county constabulary, the gendarmes, every motorist knows them. They can fine you on the spot for speeding, over-taking dangerously, or not wearing a safety-belt.

Most feared and unpopular of all are the C.R.S. (Compagnies Républicaines de la Sûreté). These mobile riot squads in their helmets and black uniforms were much in evidence during the 1968 riots, dispersing groups of students with coshes and tear-gas.

Finally there is the P.J., the 'Police Judiciaire', the French equivalent of Scotland Yard, whose headquarters on the Quai des Orfèvres are well known to every reader of Simenon's 'Maigret' stories.

Projects

1 Which is the odd man out?
   a département, commune, cité, arrondissement.
   b maire, député, fonctionnaire, préfet.

2 Which six of the following items provide money for the Mayor's budget? income tax; fees for refuse collection; entertainment tax; café licences; fee for use of slaughterhouse; gas bills; school fees; cemetery fees; driving licences; rates; marriage fees.

3 Make a list of the duties of the Mayor.

4 On which issues during his years as President did de Gaulle hold a referendum? What were the results each time?

5 On your map mark the boundaries of the 22 new regions with their regional centres. Name each region and its centre.

6 The names of two important French ministries are mentioned in the chapter. Try to make a list of as many of the others as possible, give their English equivalents, and find out what each ministry does.

7 Read a Maigret novel by Simenon (in English of course) and see if you can find anything about the P.J. and the way it works.

To discuss
Any differences between the French and British systems of government which you have discovered from this chapter. Do you think the referendum a good idea? Should we hold one in Britain, on for example, devolution or capital punishment?

For your folder
Trace a map of the départements, number them and name the chief town (chef-lieu) in each.
Collect pictures of the main government buildings in Paris.
Try to find, in newspapers and magazines, pictures of the different kinds of police.
Collect cuttings from English papers which refer to incidents in France involving the French police or government officials.

Language

The history of the French language begins with the Roman conquest of Gaul. The Romans ruled Gaul for five centuries. The 'Vulgar Latin' speech of the soldiers combined with the native language of the conquered tribes and formed the beginnings of French. The language which is spoken today gradually developed.

From the early Middle Ages until after the fall of Napoleon in the nineteenth century, French was the most widely-spoken European language. Under Louis XIV in the seventeenth century France was the most powerful nation in Europe and French became the recognised language of international diplomacy. Words such as 'embassy', 'diplomat', 'communiqué', 'negotiate', are all taken from the French.

France became a great trading nation. Traders, explorers and settlers carried the French language far beyond the borders of France and Europe.

Which do you think is the largest French-speaking city in the world, apart from Paris? The answer is Montreal, originally Mont-Réal, in Quebec. This Canadian province was first settled by the French, and even after it became part of the British Empire, the French settlers continued to speak their mother tongue, and 80% of its six million people are French-speaking.

It was a Frenchman, de la Salle, who in 1682 sailed down the Mississippi from the French possessions in Canada and claimed this part of the American continent for Louis XIV, naming it Louisiana. The jazz city of New Orleans is named after Orleans in France.

Eventually French influence spread to much of central and northern Africa, to French Guyana in South America, to Tahiti in the South Pacific and to Vietnam and Cambodia in the Far East. Martinique and Guadeloupe in the West Indies still send representatives to the French parliament.

One of the results of this colonial expansion was the spread of the French language far and wide throughout the world. A lumberjack from Quebec, a Polynesian fisherman, a cotton worker from Senegal and a Parisian businessman could all hold a conversation together in French. Their accents may be different, but they share a common world language.

Quebec

Polynesia

Senegal

Paris

Today French is either the mother tongue, an official language, or the main teaching language in over thirty countries. In world importance it is second only to English.

French influence on English

'Oyez, oyez!' the town-crier used to shout to attract attention before announcing his news. This cry comes from an old French word meaning to hear. It is just one example of French influence on the English language.

After William the Conqueror's victory at Hastings the kings of England were for more than three centuries to speak French. King Richard I, known as Richard Lionheart because of his bravery, was really a Norman, who spoke French and was called 'Cœur de Lion'. The author of the Canterbury Tales, Geoffrey Chaucer, had a French name — Chaucer was originally 'chausseur', the French for shoemaker.

Because the Norman conquerors held nearly all the positions of power in the country, many titles like 'baron', 'marquis', 'viscount' and 'duke' come from French. So do legal terms like 'judge', 'court' and 'justice', and political ones like 'reign', 'state', 'crown' and 'parliament'. The English language absorbed these new words, so that today we use them without thinking of them as anything but English.

Some words which were absorbed into English — like the word 'danse' which gave us 'dance' and 'dancing' — have been re-borrowed by the French and changed their meaning in the process. 'Le dancing' means a dance-hall in France, and oddly enough in some parts of Britain a dance-hall is called a 'palais de danse'.

'Etiquette' gave us the English word 'ticket' which the French have re-adopted as 'le ticket' and now use in preference to their own word 'le billet'.

From 'boules' we have the name for the game of bowls, while the French call the modern game of ten-pin bowling 'le bowling'.

Words which are borrowed in this way often change their sounds and spelling to make them

easier to say and write: so 'roast beef', the English version of the French words 'rôti de bœuf', has become in modern French 'le rosbif'. The dandelion is really the French word 'dent-de-lion' or lion's tooth, so called because of the shape of its leaves.

Borrowing continues in modern times. France was a pioneer in the motor-car industry, so many motoring terms are French: limousine, garage, coupé, torque. Hangar and fuselage came with the aeroplane and camouflage as a result of the fighting in the First World War.

The French are great cooks, so it is no surprise to find that we have imported a lot of cookery terms. Soufflé, meringue, nougat, casserole, purée, consommé and many others come from French.

Among the more recent borrowings are boutique and discothèque, and the world of high fashion continues to give us words like couturier, collections, salon, coiffure and so on.

Minority languages

Within France itself there are minority languages which cause problems. The most important is perhaps Breton.

In Britain in the fifth and sixth centuries the Saxons began to push the Celts further and further westwards. Many Cornish Celts fled across the channel taking their language with them. They founded the Duchy of Little Britain or Brittany, which did not become part of France until 1532. Thousands of people, mostly the older people in the west, still speak Breton. Breton, like Welsh and Gaelic, is a Celtic language and many Breton words, especially place names, have a distinct similarity to their Welsh and Cornish counterparts.

Provence too once had its own language, but apart from a few old people in the south, hardly anyone speaks it today. It was the language of the troubadours, who wandered from castle to castle singing and reciting their poetry. 'Ballade' is one Provençal word which has passed into both French and English. Others are 'beret', 'bastille' and 'nougat'.

Also in the south, but this time in a small area on either side of the Western Pyrenees, 'Euskara' the language of the Basques is still spoken by half a million Spanish Basques and nearly a hundred thousand French ones. The Basques are a proud people, renowned as soldiers and sailors, who have retained not only their own language but their own customs and even their own sport, pelota.

At the Mediterranean end of the Pyrenees another language bridges the border between France and Spain — Catalan. This is spoken from

Above: *Le franglais*
Left: *Part of the Bayeux tapestry*

57

Perpignan in France to Barcelona, the Catalonian capital, and as far south as Valencia. It is also a language you might hear spoken on the holiday islands of Majorca, Minorca and Ibiza.

Le Franglais

One of the English-speaking world's most successful exports is its language, and one of the chief importers is France.

A young 'teenager' does 'le shopping' at 'le weekend'. She eats 'un sandwich' in 'un snack-bar' or 'un self-service'. In the evening she meets 'le boyfriend' to go to 'le Pop-club' where 'les fans' listen to 'le Hit-Parade' as they drink 'un coke'.

This mixture of French and English was christened 'le franglais' by a French professor who is very worried about the threat to his beloved language. Some French people think it superior, 'très snob', to use English words and phrases. Many English expressions are used instead of perfectly good French ones with just the same meaning. Why say 'le self-service' instead of 'libre service'? Why 'faire le shopping' instead of 'faire les courses'?

There is an explanation for this trend. After the Second World War thousands of American

troops remained in France. Some married French wives and are still there. They had their own radio stations which helped to produce an international pop-culture based on American and British stars. Continental teenagers learned some of their English by singing Elvis Presley's songs. They wore 'le blue-jeans' and 'le T-shirt', danced 'le rock-'n-roll' and 'le twist' and ate 'le chewing-gum' and 'les cornflakes'.

The original European way of life became Americanised with supermarkets, snack-bars, motels and drug-stores. Television brought American programmes into French homes.

Now in the seventies British and American influence continues to grow. International firms are often under American control. Chrysler has taken over both Rootes and Simca, and the big oil companies use American words like 'le tanker', 'le gas-oil', 'le pipe-line'. The increase in travel facilities and communications means that newly-coined words pass quickly from country to country and from continent to continent.

Much of the new space-age technology is American-inspired, and many scientific and technical terms passing into French are from the American. Examples are 'le lift-off', 'le feed-back', 'le transistor', and there are hundreds of others.

France sees yet another threat to her language in Britain's entry into the E.E.C. English has become an official language of the community. Ambitious French youngsters must know it well if they wish to make a successful career in industry or commerce.

What are the French doing about this linguistic invasion? The French Academy — one of whose

Sappa

A Paris 'drug-store'

constant tasks is to revise the dictionary of the French language and keep it up to date — recently issued a list of native French equivalents of American and English terms which are heard everywhere. Civil servants and schools and colleges are urged to use the genuine French expression. For instance they are instructed to use:

l'ingénierie NOT l'engineering
le pétrolier NOT le tanker
le palmarès NOT le hit-parade

l'industrie du spectacle NOT le show-business
l'homme d'affaires NOT le businessman
le tourne-disque NOT le pickup.

Will the radio, the television and the press continue to use the imported words? And if they do, what will be the result? Language is a living thing. It changes all the time — we do not speak the language of Chaucer, of Shakespeare, or even of our great-grandparents. Language grows but it can also die. What will be the fate of French?

Projects

1 Who are these famous people connected with Quebec? Jacques Cartier, Pierre Trudeau, Samuel de Champlain.

2 These expressions have been borrowed from the English but have changed their meanings. Find out what they now mean in French: le smoking, le parking, le pressing, le footing.

3 Here are some French expressions which are sometimes used in English. What do they mean? rendezvous, au revoir, à propos, au pair, entente cordiale, savoir faire, aide-de-camp.

4 Guess which English words these originally were. The French have borrowed them and changed their spelling. le biftek, le bébé, hourra, le paquebot, le boulingrin, le redingote, le bouledozeur, le bouledogue, le pique-nique.

5 Many words have come into both French and English from former colonies. Here are some French examples. What are the English equivalents? le bambou, la banane, le canoë, le hamac, le cacao, l'ouragan, le tabac, le chimpanzée. Now try to think of some more English words from the Third World and see if the French words are the same.

7 Mark in on a map of France those areas where a French dialect or a language other than French is spoken.

6 Look at a map of North America. Trace the area of French settlement by looking for places with French names in Louisiana and along the Mississippi to Quebec.

8 Look at a page of a French magazine and write down all the English words or expressions which you recognise.

9 Look at the top twenty hit parade in France. How many non-French songs/groups are there? Compare this with the top twenty in Britain (if possible in the same week).

To discuss
Do you think Breton or Welsh can survive as a language? Do you think it important that it should?
Would you like to see an international language, for example Esperanto taught in all our schools?
Is it necessary for the British to learn a foreign language?

For your folder
Any tickets, letters, advertisements etc. where instructions and/or information are printed in more than one language. Cut out any advertisements from French magazines, which are about British/American products, or which use English expressions.

Holidays

About half the French, perhaps twenty-five million people, go on holiday every year. Everyone has the right to a month's paid leave from work. Schools throughout France all break up at the same time. This means that two thirds of the French start their holidays between the last week in July and the first week in August. Accommodation is scarce and expensive. The roads are jammed and dangerous. Something like four thousand holidaymakers die in road accidents each year. The French have a special phrase to describe this holiday fever: they call it 'le grand départ'.

In August, Paris is abandoned by most of its inhabitants. It is taken over by tourists, who often have difficulty in shopping and finding accommodation and entertainment, for many shopkeepers and hoteliers are on holiday themselves. Some cafés and restaurants, and all theatres are closed. Many Parisians visit their families in the provinces for there are many Bretons and Auvergnats working in or owning hotels, restaurants, cafés or bars in Paris. In fact about 40% of the French spend their holidays visiting friends or relatives. Of those who do not have a holiday, the majority are farmers or agricultural workers, retired people, or low-paid manual workers.

France itself is an ideal country for holidays. Even nowadays few Frenchmen see much good reason for spending a holiday outside France and only a small proportion do so. France has after all the best food in the world, wine, sunshine, splendid and varied scenery, and 2,700 kilometres of wonderful coastline.

Donnezan – Rapho

Top: *How the French spend their holidays*
Bottom: *The 'grand départ'*

In fact over half the holidays taken in France are spent somewhere along that coastline, probably in the south. The French Riviera is famous throughout the world. One of the main streets in Nice is the Promenade des Anglais, so-called because it was popular with the English aristocracy at the turn of the century. Cannes is well known for its film festival, and Brigitte Bardot made St-Tropez famous. The newly developed tourist area in the Roussillon, and the island of Corsica are two other popular regions in the south.

Government money has helped the tourist industry in seaside and country alike. Many villages in the Alps and Pyrenees were isolated and poor a few years ago. They are now being developed as ski resorts.

More and more people can afford a winter break as well as a summer holiday, and the mountains of the Jura, the Massif Central and the Vosges provide a different kind of holiday and perhaps a more restful one than the seaside resorts.

Spain and Italy are the most popular countries for holidays abroad. France has a common border with each of these countries, so it is easy for a French family to motor there. Package tours on charter flights tend to take holidaymakers further afield, to Greece or Yugoslavia or to former French colonies in Africa like Morocco and Tunisia.

Many French teenagers have spent holidays in West Germany, and at very low cost. The Franco-German youth treaty signed in 1963 provides for subsidised travel between the two countries in the hope that lasting friendships and real understanding will grow up between the young people of the two nations.

Resorts like Brighton, Bournemouth and Eastbourne on the south coast of England swarm with French teenagers in the summer months. Why do they come to Britain? Surely not because of the climate! Most of them in fact will be hoping to improve their English at one of the many language schools in this part of the country. Their parents, especially their mothers, could well be shopping in London for clothes which are still cheaper here than in France. Many French people used to come over on day trips to places like Dover or Folkestone where they could buy food, especially meat and butter, so much more cheaply than at home. Despite the cost of the cross-channel ferry, and the escalating prices in Britain, it still costs them less to do their shopping here. And of course, many come purely as tourists to visit places like Cambridge, Edinburgh, Canterbury, (or even perhaps Hastings!).

French Government Tourist Office

Many French holidays are organised on a group basis. School children go to 'colonies' or 'centres de vacances', youth camps which are run by monitors. British students anxious to improve their French often act as monitors. In winter, for those children lucky enough to get a place, there are the 'classes de neige' in the mountains.

Above: A 'classe de neige'

Adults can also have their holidays organised. The 'Club Méditerranée' specialises in small holiday villages. The accommodation is often basic in individual cottages or huts, the holiday makers usually eat together in the communal restaurant. and there are organised activities like excursions and sports.

Many large firms have their own holiday centres for their employees. Peugeot, the car firm, have five holiday estates for workers' children, two holiday camps for 14 to 18 year-olds, and a residential home for retired workers.

Most weekends from early spring right through to late autumn there are huge traffic jams in Paris and on the main roads — on Friday evening as the weekenders set out and even more so on Sunday evening as they return. There are constant news flashes on the radio giving the latest traffic situation so that motorists can avoid the worst jams. Many of these Parisians are escaping to a weekend cottage or 'pavillon' in the country, where the family has more room than in a confined flat in the capital.

Windenberger – Rapho

If a public holiday like May 1st or August 15th happens to fall on a Thursday, the French will often 'faire le pont', that is, make a bridge over the intervening Friday by making that day a holiday too, so that they can enjoy a long weekend away from the bustle of city life.

Deciding where to stay can be a problem. For young people there is often a youth hostel in the region they want to visit. Hotels are usually too expensive for them. These are graded from one to four stars and on top of these there is a de-luxe category. This official grading fixes the prices which they are allowed to charge and most of them are listed in one of the three main

Top: *Weekend cottage in the country*
Middle: *A 2-star hotel*
Bottom: *Camp site*

tourist guides: Michelin, which has the biggest selection, the 'Logis de France' which lists the smaller hotels often off the beaten track, and the 'Routier' guide to economical overnight stops for long-distance lorry drivers. It is useful to remember that hotel charges are on a room basis — you pay for the room, whether you occupy one bed or all the beds in it.

If you are staying in a hotel for at least three days you can cut costs by asking for 'demi-pension': bed, breakfast and evening meal. You will probably only need a picnic lunch at mid-day, but if you do decide you want a good, cheap lunch, it's often best to follow a lorry driver into a 'Relais des Routiers', where the quality of the food is excellent and may well surprise you.

Finally, many French people solve their holiday problem by camping. Camping is very well organised in France, and most holiday towns have their municipal camp sites which are often very good indeed. Sites are graded and the best of them offer outstandingly good facilities: hot and cold showers, all modern conveniences, shops, sometimes even their own swimming-pool. The Frenchman in any case usually likes to take all his home comforts with him when on holiday, and a French family, even when they are only out for a day in the country, will take their folding table and chairs, kettle and stove, and often the most elaborate picnic food.

If you want to spend a holiday in France, decide whereabouts you would like to go and write to the local information office, the 'Syndicat d'Initiative'. Almost all towns have one. It will supply town guides, brochures and information on accommodation.

Wherever you go, and whatever type of holiday in France you choose, bon voyage et bon retour!

1 Each strip of coastline has a special name. Find out where the following are and label them on your map.
a)Côte d'Emeraude, b)Côte d'Azur, c)Côte d'Opale, d)Côte d'Argent, e)Côte Vermeille.
Insert the names of the chief resorts in each. Can you find any other names for parts of the French coast?

2 If you are interested in the following activities, name a place in France where you would expect to enjoy a holiday.
a)ski-ing, b)sailing, c)sun-bathing, d)looking at old buildings, e)exploring ancient or prehistoric sites.

3 Find out where as many as possible of the places on French postage stamps are situated and insert any stamps you have on to a map. What is interesting about these places? Why were they chosen to figure on the stamps?

4 Write to a Syndicat d'Initiative for brochures and hotel information. (Send an international reply coupon if you want to be sure of a reply.) Then plan, and work out the cost of, a holiday in your chosen area.

5 Make a diagram showing the various ways in which the French spend their holidays.

6 Try to get hold of a French camp-site guide. Copy the symbols which show what you can expect to find in the camp of your choice.

7 Find out as much as you can about festivals in France and places of pilgrimage.

To discuss
Where would be the most interesting area in which to spend a holiday in France?
The relative merits of camping and a holiday in a seaside hotel.
What makes the French Riviera such an interesting and popular place?

For your folder
Pictures from travel brochures, post cards, stamps and post-marks, travel articles from newspapers and magazines dealing with France, and maps from travel firms.

Supplementary books and materials

European Schoolbooks have a very large range of books and audio-visual aids covering every aspects of France and French civilisation. New material is being published all the time. The following list represents only a small selection of core titles, which together could form a resource base for French Studies.

Books

Petit Larousse
Revised yearly, the best one-volume encyclopedic dictionary available.

Nouveau Guide France
A mine of information about France, her institutions and way of life.

France
Published by Documentation Française, the official French Government publishers, this volume gives a general view of the main areas of French life, illustrated throughout in colour. Available in French or English, and regularly up-dated.

Guide Bleu France
Latest edition of a famous and comprehensive guidebook. Regional guides are also published in the same series.

Comment vivent les français
Contains many useful and well-designed tables and diagrams, and is at the same time in simple enough French to be accessible to "O" level pupils.

Visual Aids

Flannelgraph map of France
A large outline map (120 x 120 cm) printed on raised drape, with sheets of topic figurines. Topics published or planned are: Placenames, rivers and mountains; Food and drink; Holidays and Tourism; Industry; Historic buildings and sites; Transport and communications; Agriculture and weather; Regional costumes and festivals.

Carte de France illustrée
A large bright map, full of interesting details for pupils to explore.

Blackboard map of France
An outline map on a dark plastic surface suitable for writing on with chalk of all colours; easily cleaned.

Rubber stamp map of France
Produces an outline map, 13 x 16 cm, for the cost of a sheet of plain paper. Ideal for project assignments, and for testing.

Regardons la France
105 colour slides in three broad sections: history; physical geography; daily life. A booklet of teaching notes is included.

For more detailed information and resources on the individual topics covered in *This is France*: please refer to European Schoolbooks' current French catalogue, which presents a wide range of books and materials arranged by topics.

Some useful addresses

Centre for Information on Language Teaching
20 Carlton House Terrace, London SW1

French Embassy
Services de Presse et d'Information, 58 Knightsbridge, London SW1
Service Culturel, 22 Wilton Crescent, London SW1

French Government Tourist Office
178 Piccadilly, London W1

Institut Français
15 Queensbury Place, London SW7

Schools Information Unit,
Centre for Contemporary European Studies, University of Sussex, Falmer, Brighton

Central Bureau for Educational Visits and Exchanges,
43 Dorset Street, London W1